ON DATING AND MATING

- On the question of which came first, the chicken or the egg: In one particular case, most definitely the chicken. A single cock, in a 1937 study, was observed to copulate 53 times in one day.

- On the matter of dancing to a different beat: A 1984 study reports that high-level noise, such as that frequently found in discos, causes homosexuality in mice and deafness among pigs.

- On how to promote safe sex: In 1976 it was found that the incidence of gonorrhea had declined in Sweden, but not in Denmark. The reason: while the Swedes have a simple word for prophylactics, ``kondom,'' the Danish equivalent is ``sanger-skabsforebyggende middel.''

DRUNKEN GOLDFISH

GOLDFISH

& Other Irrelevant Scientific Research

William Hartston

FAWCETT CREST • NEW YORK

Contents

Knowledge in Depth

The idea for this book began when I came across a research paper about the effect of alcohol on the ability of goldfish to remember things. Fascinated, I delved deeper into the topic and discovered several other papers on the same, or closely related themes. Following up footnotes and references I then found one which explained the effect of alcohol on neurotic dogs. (In properly regulated doses, it can cure them of premature ejaculation.) Rejecting anything that looked to me like mainstream science, I continued to add to my collection. The result is this book.

The main subject areas stemmed naturally from my rather haphazard method of gathering research. I must be one of the few people who regularly visit the University Library in Cambridge in order simply to browse. I am certainly the only one who sits in the reading room, turning the pages of current academic journals and cackling with laughter. Once promising topics are identified with serendipity, I then try to research in more detail. Much research, unfortunately, is inaccessible to all but the specialist. That, more than anything, has restricted the range of this book. If it seems to be dominated by animals, psychology, sociology and sex, it is perhaps due to the ready accessibility of these subjects to the layman. It may also be due to the personal tastes of the author.

In laying out the material, I have followed the lead set by the current edition of Encyclopaedia Britannica, with long articles on the major areas of research (Goldfish, Alcohol, Sex, etc.), then shorter entries arranged alphabetically on the less important topics. The whole work is fully cross-referenced and each article on a major topic is followed by a list of references. These include not only works referred to in the preceding text, but also suggestions for further reading. Most of these the author has himself not yet read, but the titles look promising anyway.

If there is any serious intent in this book, which on the whole is unlikely, it should be sought in either of two directions. Firstly, I should like to draw to the attention of a wider readership some aspects of human knowledge and achievement which have been lying too long on the dusty shelves of academic libraries. There is knowledge here too fascinating—and not only to prematurely ejaculating dogs—to be left to the world of academe. The effect drinking the blood of a schizophrenic has on spiders and their webs; which parts of the human body contribute most greatly to self-esteem; why rats drown more quickly if you shave their whiskers off; these and so many other pieces of knowledge deserve a larger audience.

The second potentially serious aspect of this work is just to drop a gentle hint that there might be too much research going on, and much of that is taken far too seriously. I have nothing but admiration for dedicated researchers, and I have no wish to criticize their work as useless. No doubt much of

great value has come out of apparently inconsequential research. But it must be admitted that a great deal of space on
shelves is occupied by dissertations and theses which add
very little to worthwhile knowledge. A post-graduate project
may be excellent training in the methodology of research,
but thereafter, destined to be read by an average 1.6 people,
can seem little more than a waste of paper.

It has been said that research is only idleness by another
name. There is much evidence in this book to support such
a claim, but I would not totally agree. The true researcher is
motivated solely by curiosity. The usefulness or applicability
of the results is not, and cannot be, an important factor gov-
erning the directions of the research. Many results of high
potential value will be found in these pages, the work of
dedicated men and women of admirable curiosity, destined
to be ignored because their results are lost, buried under the
morass of mainstream research.

The author's position is thus ambiguous: on the one hand
I have great admiration and love of research for its own sake;
on the other, I cannot help feeling that there is far too much
of it going on. I must stress to any of the authors quoted in
these pages who may come across the references of their
work, that the quotes come not with any implied criticism
but with high esteem and fondness.

I must thank not only the Cambridge University Library
for filling itself with such a mountain of irrelevant knowledge, but also my academic friends who, while stoutly main-
taining the value of their own research projects, were always
so willing to rat on their colleagues. I should also like to
acknowledge a debt to the Journal of Irreproducible Results,
which has made such fine efforts to give occasional promi-

nence to works of similarly irrelevant research. I have found many useful references in their pages.

Above all this book has been an experiment, exploring the possibility of bringing together unrelated pieces of work from the backwaters of scientific research. Perhaps some day the solitary paddlers in those backwaters will get together to form an Institute for the Stagnation of Science, with its own multidisciplinary journal. If any reader has contributions to make (his own research or that of colleagues) to the fund of irrelevant research, offprints or detailed references will be most welcome and should be sent to the author, marked "Proc. Inst. Stag. Sci." c/o Unwin Hyman, 40 Museum Street, London, WC1.

If enough of you can contribute, I might even get an effortless sequel out of it.

William R. Hartston
Cambridge, 1987

Part One

Fluid Dynamics

In this section we shall concentrate on two important fluids—alcohol and water—and things that move about and die in those fluids.

The first chapter concerns alcohol and its effects on men, women, dogs and goldfish, among others. The theme of goldfish is continued

. . . things that move about and die in those fluids . . .

in the second chapter, while chapter three is devoted mainly to the antics of the dog-drowners of the Royal Medical and Chirurgical Society of London in 1862.

For those who wish to keep up with research in related fields, the following journals can be recommended:

The Journal of Fish Biology
The Journal of Fish Diseases
Fish Farming International
Fish Traders' Weekly
Fried Fish Caterer, which changed its name in 1975 to:
  Friers' Catering Advertiser
Research Advances in Alcohol and Drug Problems
International Journal on Alcohol and Alcoholism
British Journal on Alcohol and Alcoholism
Alcohol and Drug Research
Proceedings of the Society for the Study and Cure of Inebriety, which changed its name in 1887 to:
Proceedings of the Society for the Study of Inebriety, then changed it again in 1903 to:
British Journal of Inebriety, then finally in 1946 changed to *British Journal of Addiction*
Notes on Water Research
Water Research (formerly the *International Journal of Air and Water Pollution*)
Aqualine Abstracts.

Chapter One

Alcohol

"It provokes the desire, but it takes away the performance."

Macbeth, Act II, sc. iii.

The effects of alcohol on lechery received a useful airing in the exchange between Macduff and a porter in Shakespeare's play, though the matter was not properly researched for another three centuries. More of that later. It is proper scientific style to begin with lower life forms and progress later to humans, so we shall also follow that path.

There are undoubted methodological difficulties in conducting proper research into the effects of alcohol addiction, whether these effects be on dogs, mice, humans or other animals. One researcher reported difficulty in controlling the volume of alcohol intake because his mouse subjects kept getting drunk and falling asleep. Others have found human subjects no more reliable. Mentioning some research on the social effects of chronic drinking, V. J. Adesso (1980— "Experimental Studies of Human Drinking Behavior") observes: "In studies of prolonged drinking . . . self-reports of sexual feelings and observed sexual behavior increased during drinking." He goes on to add: "The alcoholics in these studies were typically unable to recall these changes after the drinking period."

So there are certain problems in working with drunks. A major problem with animals, however, is turning them into drunks in the first place. "It is notoriously difficult," wrote J. L. Falk in 1980, "to induce animals to drink sufficient ethanol chronically to become physically dependent on it."

Bearing in mind the problems associated with this area of research, we are now ready to stagger through some of the findings.

THE EFFECTS OF ALCOHOL ON DOGS

M. K. Petrova (1945) observed differences in alcohol-related behavior among different "neural types" of dog. Ten dogs, of different temperaments, were offered a drink of milk laced with alcohol. Only the "weaker dogs" were reported to succumb to the temptation, whereafter they soon showed signs of extreme excitement or they fell asleep. Another dog displayed symptoms suggesting alcoholic hallucinations. Old

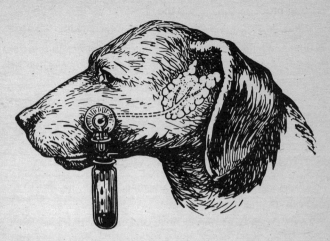

The old-fashioned brandy cask was more fun.

dogs, ''exhausted after many years of experimental work,'' were affected most by the continued use of alcohol.

These largely anecdotal results can hardly be considered a properly controlled experiment, but Gantt (1952) provided some hard facts for hard-drinking canines. Restricting his observations to the effect of alcohol on the sexual reflexes of normal and neurotic male dogs, he made two important discoveries:

1. *Alcohol has a depressant effect on a dog's sexual reflexes in proportion to its dose: large doses completely abolish the sexual reflex.*
2. *In regulated doses, alcohol may have a therapeutic effect on certain neurotic conditions of the dog, such as ejaculatio praecox.*

Yes, it's true: alcohol, properly administered, can cure your dog of premature ejaculation.

Before we rush into the treatment, however, we should pause to consider another important question: Do dogs suffer from hangovers? This topic is thoroughly discussed by G. Freund in his 1979 paper "Comparison of Alcohol Dependence, Withdrawal and Hangover in Humans and Animals." His work forms the basis of our next section.

DO ANIMALS HAVE HANGOVERS?

The evidence overwhelmingly suggests that the answer to that question is "yes."

In chronically alcoholic mice and rats, withdrawal from alcohol has been associated with the following symptoms: tail stiffening, teeth chattering, hair standing on end, wet shakes, broad-based gait, tremors, bizarre behavior, backing up cage walls, sudden propulsion, sudden vocalizations, convulsions, whole-body rigidity.

Cats which had been force-fed ethanol for five weeks, then removed from the diet, showed pupil dilation, salivation, tremors in all four limbs, and restlessness. They were startled by small noises and afraid of people.

Dogs coming off alcohol were much the same, though Essig and Lam (1968) observed that one dog "developed hallucinatory behavior during the 64th hour of withdrawal. If not distracted the dog would move its head as if looking at a moving object not visible to human observers." It also snapped its jaw and tried to bite whatever it was looking at. This behavior went on for 40 hours during which the dog slept very little.

Monkeys showed tremors, rigid movements while walk-

They were willing to try anything to cure the dog's premature ejaculations.

ing, spontaneous body twitches and jerks, salivation, pupil dilation, retching and vomiting. Chimpanzees showed irritability, sweaty palms and feet, fear of light, quick breathing and rigidity. Fever and convulsions were also noted.

So, on the whole, you might prefer to let your dog keep his premature ejaculations rather than risk the consequences of his becoming addicted to alcohol.

All this makes you wonder why people would put alcohol in the goldfish water. They are concerned, however, not with premature ejaculation or hangovers, but with learning.

THE EFFECTS OF ALCOHOL ON THE LEARNING ABILITIES OF THE GOLDFISH

Goldfish immersed in 3.1% alcohol will overturn (lose the righting reflex) within six to eight minutes. Because of this

Five fish regretting imbibing that last little drink.

tendency to fall over when drunk, the goldfish is a good model for research on the effects of alcohol. When preliminary studies in 1968 and 1969 indicated that goldfish tended to forget things when drunk, and that Siamese Fighting Fish became more aggressive after a little drink or two, their attraction as experimental animals became irresistible. (It should also be mentioned that you can cut out a great deal of the goldfish brain without impairing its memory. This is a useful option to have in memory research.) Finally, leaving a goldfish stewing in alcoholic water is one way to ensure that its blood alcohol level is maintained at a known concentration.

The first important result concerns the effect of alcoholic blackouts. R. S. Ryback, in his classic 1969 paper ''The Use of Goldfish as a Model for Alcohol Amnesia in Man'' (*Quarterly J. Studies on Alcohol*, 30, 877–82), gave the fish a simple learning task. In a mildly alcoholic solution, they were taught to turn in a particular direction (left or right) in a Y-shaped maze. Once training was successfully completed, some of the fish were removed to a high-alcohol solution where they stayed for an hour. The fish soon looked sluggish and some turned over on their sides within the hour.

Three days later, all the fish were tested again in the same mildly alcoholic water of the training sessions. Those who had never tasted strong drink remembered their learning task excellently. Those who had blacked out forgot it, while those who had sampled the heavy liquor without collapsing also retained most of their learning.

So a mildly inebriated goldfish will remember what you teach it, unless it continues drinking until it is paralytic.

Further experiments by Ryback demonstrated that goldfish memory is state-dependent, i.e., its ability to recall something depends on the state of the water being the same as that in which it was first trained. So if you teach a goldfish something sober, it may well forget it when drunk; but if you teach it something when it is intoxicated, it will forget it when it has sobered up. Amazingly, the same result has been shown to hold for humans, whose ability to recall lists of words or nonsense-syllables depends in the same manner upon their alcoholic states at time of recall and memorization being the same.

If you really want to confuse a goldfish, however, you have to devise an experiment which involves both short-term and long-term memory. Ryback (1976) trained fish to escape from a dark box by choosing the right-hand (or right-fin) door of a two-door exit. When this behavior was firmly established, the ''correct'' door was reversed. For a short series of trials, the left door became the way out. The fish soon learned the new rules. When given a free choice of door after a further five-minute delay, most intoxicated fish continued to choose the left side. But if the fish were then removed and brought

. . . if you really want to confuse a fish . . .

back in an hour, their choice reverted to the original (right) door. These results suggest that alcohol intoxication temporarily facilitates short-term memory, but that long-term memory will reassert itself after sufficient time.

Some of these as well as other studies also showed that small doses of alcohol can initially enhance performance at learning tasks. *The mildly inebriated goldfish learned their correct maze habits more quickly than sober fish.* A similar observation about humans had been noted by Kraepelin in 1892, though for both humans and goldfish the result is believed only to hold true for simple learning tasks.

For those worried about potential hangovers in the goldfish, we should mention that a review of the literature shows that juvenile goldfish are less sensitive to alcohol's depressive or inhibitory effects than adult goldfish.

ALCOHOL IN RATS, MICE AND FLIES

We briefly summarize some further results before finally returning to human alcoholics. With rats, mice and flies, as with humans, there is liable to be confusion as to whether they actually enjoy alcohol, or whether it is getting drunk which is the main object of the drinking. Kahn and Stellar (1960) accordingly experimented on normal rats and rats which had been deprived of their sense of smell. It was found that the ability to smell made rats prefer lower concentrations of alcohol and they thus drank less of it. The rats which could not smell just drank on happily.

A similar experiment was done on blowflies, which had their antennae and taste organs removed, so that they could not distinguish alcohols by smell or taste. Their response to different alcohols was then measured by taking note of their proboscis response to stimulation of their torsal receptors. The results are too technical to go into here. Instead we return briefly to rats to mention that *if a rat is exposed to alcohol prenatally its nipple attachment after birth tends to be prolonged.*

Mice are more complex. According to McClearn and

Rodgers (1961), a mouse's tendency towards alcoholism is controlled by more than a single gene.

ALCOHOL AND HUMANS

When A. E. Carver wrote about "The Interrelationship of Sex and Alcohol" in 1948, he concluded that:

> . . . with cultural restraints removed, an adolescent girl may be easy prey to seduction . . . but large doses of alcohol may be required in homosexuality and incest.

Modern research has done little to upset these findings, but has concentrated on the effects of those large doses of alcohol on behavior. We shall concentrate still further on the effects on sexual behavior.

Following Abel and Blanchard (1976), we can assert that penile tumescence is a reliable measure of sexual arousal in males. Females are more of a problem, but vaginal blood volume and pressure pulse are found to be equally reliable here. In several studies, subjects were administered alcohol (given a drink) and then exposed to sexually stimulating material (shown dirty pictures). Their arousal was objectively measured as described above.

The findings show that physiological sexual arousal decreases with the imbibing of alcohol. The effects of this result are, however, obscured by another finding which shows that for females, physiological sexual arousal correlates negatively with subjective sexual arousal. In other words, the randier a woman thinks she is, the less she is really. This is hard to believe, but if true, it would suggest that plying a woman with drink, and thereby reducing her true arousal, would be a good way to increase her subjective arousal.

A further defect of all this research, is that its concentration on arousal neglects the question of performance. It has, however, been shown (J. A. Viamontes "Sexual depressant effect of alcohol" *Med. Aspects, Hum. Sex.* 1975, 9, 31) that alcohol does impair the sexual performance of alcoholics. On the other hand, it has also been suggested (Lang et al.: "Effects of alcohol on aggression in male social drinkers," *J. Abnormal Psychol.* 1975, 84, 508–18) that the apparent disinhibiting effect of alcohol allows a misattribution of the responsibility of deviant acts performed while intoxicated. In other words, you can have a good time when you're drunk without feeling so guilty about it.

The whole area is riddled with uncertainty. More research is clearly needed. (The present author is available for the price of a crate of good claret.)

REFERENCES

Agranoff, B. W. and Klinger, P. O. (1964). "Puromycin effect on memory fixation in the goldfish." *Science*, 146, 952–3.

Briddell, D. W. and Wilson, G. T. (1976). "The effects of alcohol and expectancy set on male sexual arousal." *J. Abnormal Psychology*, 85, 225–34.

Carver, A. E. (1948). "The interrelationship of sex and alcohol." *Int. J. Sexology*, 2, 78–81.

Dethier, V. G. and Chadwick, L. E. (1946). "Rejection thresholds of the blowfly for a series of aliphatic alcohols." 1946 *Publ. Bd.*, No. 47071.

Essig, C. F. and Lam, R. C. (1968). "Convulsions and hallucinatory behaviour following alcohol withdrawal in the dog." *Arch. Neurol.*, 18, 626-32.

Freund, G. (1969). "Alcohol withdrawal syndrome in mice." *Arch. Neurol.*, 21, 315–20.

Gantt, W. H. (1952). "Effect of alcohol on the sexual reflexes of normal and neurotic male dogs." *Psychosom. Medicine*, 14, 174–81.

Goldstein, D. B. (1975). "Physical dependence on alcohol in mice." *Fed. Proc.*, 34, 1953–61.

Ingle, D. J. (1965). "The use of the fish in neuropsychology." *Perspectives in Biology and Medicine*, 8, 241–60.

Lester, D. (1961). "Self-maintenance of intoxication in the rat." *Quarterly J. Stud. Alcohol*, 22, 223–31.

Kahn, M. and Stellar, E. (1960). "Alcohol preference in normal and anosmic rats." *J. Comp. Physiol. Psychology, 53, 571–5.*

McClearn, G. and Rodgers, D. A. (1961). "Genetic factors in alcohol preference of laboratory mice." J. Comp. Physiol. Psychology, 54, 116–119.

Masserman, J. H. and Yum, K. S. (1946). "An analysis of the influence of alcohol on experimental neurosis in cats." *Psychosom. Medicine*, 8, 36–52.

Mello, N. K. (1973). "A review of methods to induce alcohol addiction in animals." *Pharmacol. Biochem. Behav.*, 1, 89–101.

Moskowitz, H. and Burns, M. (1976). "Effects of rate of drinking on human performance." *Journal of Studies on Alcohol*, 37, 598–605.

Petrova, M. K. (1945). "Effect of chronic use of alcohol on the higher nervous activity of dogs." *Trud. Fiziol. Lab. Pavlov.*, 1945.

Riley, Bunis and Greenfield (1984). "Nipple attachment in neonatal rats exposed to alcohol prenatally." *Bull. Psychom. Soc.*, 22.

Ryback, R. S. (1970). "The use of fish, especially goldfish, in alcohol research." *Quarterly J. Studies on Alcohol*, 31, 162–6.

Ryback, R. S. (1976). "A method to study short-term memory in the goldfish." *Pharmacology, Biochemistry and Behaviour*, 4, 489–91.

Proceedings of the Society for the Study of Inebriety.

Shupe, L. (1954). "Alcohol and crime. A study of the urine alcohol concentrations found in 882 persons arrested during or immediately after the commission of a felony." *J. Criminal Law, Criminology and Police Science*, 44, 661–4.

Wilson, G. T. and Lawson, D. M. (197a). "Expectancies, alcohol and sexual arousal in male social drinkers." *J. Abnormal Psychology*, 85, 587–94.

Wilson, G. T. and Lawson, D. M. (1976b). "The effects of alcohol on sexual arousal in women." *J. Abnormal Psychology*, 85, 489–97.

Wilson, G. T. and Lawson, D. M. (1978). "Expectancies, alcohol, and sexual arousal in women." *J. Abnormal Psychology*, 87, 358–67.

Wilson, G. T., Lawson, D. M. and Abrams, D. B. (1978). "Effects of alcohol on sexual arousal in male alcoholics." *J. Abnormal Psychology*, 87, 609–16.

Yano, K., Rhoads, G. G. and Kagan, A. (1977). "Coffee,

alcohol and risk of coronary heart disease among Japanese men living in Hawaii.'' *New England J. Medicine*, 297, 405–9.

Chapter Two

Goldfish

The role of goldfish in research has been clearly established in the previous chapter, but their value to science lies not only in their capacity to fall over when drunk. The goldfish has a convenient brain to study: it is a small brain in a large cranial carapace, so injections into the brain are easily managed. Further than that, its visual abilities, swimming habits and sexual behavior have also been the subject of numerous research projects. What follows is only a brief ripple on the surface of the water in the bowl of goldfish research.

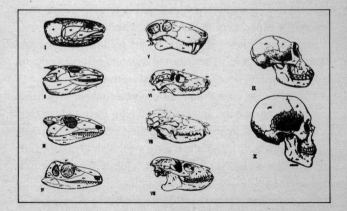

How a fish skull evolves into a human skull in ten easy stages.

THE GOLDFISH BRAIN

Goldfish may not seem very bright, but they are willing learners. We have already referred to the goldfish's ability to learn which way to turn in a Y-shaped maze, or whether to go through a right-hand or left-hand door, but there are other things the experimenter can teach his fish. (Incidentally–*it has been shown that the learning ability of the goldfish is at its maximum in the months January–March.* Its mental capacities are at their poorest in the summer months after spawning.)

Shasoua's (1968) goldfish had small polystyrene floats attached to their chins. They then had to learn to swim in a manner which compensated for the weight of the float. This experiment was done in order to see if changes could be measured in the RNA synthesized in the goldfish brain during the learning process. (To understand why this is important the reader is referred to the chapter on Worms.) Each goldfish had been injected with a radioactive label in its brain before the experiment in order to monitor activity.

Initially, of course, the floats on the goldfish chins caused them to overtopple. They started swimming upside down, but within a few hours learned to swim normally.

This gives the clue to another useful technique in goldfish learning experiments. Instead of teaching them to turn right or left, some researchers have taught them to swim ''standing up'' in the water. If, after teaching a goldfish to compensate for having a weight on its chin, the chin weight is then removed, the goldfish will start swimming upright. It still compensates for the non-existent float. Eventually it resumes its normal posture, but not until the experimenters have no doubt collected much valuable data.

GOLDFISH VISION

Ingle (1985) did some good work on the color vision mechanism of the goldfish. *Three goldfish were trained to approach a particular color within a richly colored but variable Mondrian background.* Then the background lighting was radically changed. The goldfish still recognized which color they were meant to swim toward. The findings indicate that goldfish recognize colors in much the same way as humans, by comparison with the background, rather than by a pure analysis of the spectrum of light reflected by the object.

No work has yet been done to see if goldfish prefer other artists to Mondrian. Perhaps some are really Klee fish.

Of course, if you blind the goldfish first, they won't recognize any colors. Neither, according to Timms (1976), will they swim so fast. In order to discover the role of monocular and binocular vision on their swimming behavior, normal goldfish, one-eyed goldfish and blinded goldfish were observed swimming, and their angles of turn, frequency of turning, and speed monitored.

The results showed that one-eyed goldfish swim as fast as two-eyed goldfish, but blind goldfish are slower. The one-eyed goldfish, however, has a strong bias towards turning in the direction of the blind side. This is curious because most other animals with only one eye tend to turn towards the sighted side.

If you don't blind your goldfish, you can discover fascinating things about their visual abilities: they can distinguish between circles whose diameters differ by as little as three millimetres (Rowley, 1934), and their response to standard optical illusions is very similar to that of man (Herter, 1930).

. . . Octopuses are rewarded for attacking the correct object . . .

At this stage, we should like to diverge a little from gold-fish to bring in the octopus. This is mainly because the chapter would otherwise be too short, and also to boost the reference list by adding N. S. Sutherland's marvelous series of papers.

The octopus (plural: octopuses, or the archaic octopodes, but never octopi, which is simply wrong) has a very interesting brain, especially for the study of visual responses and shape discrimination. Sutherland (1960) showed that octopuses were better at discriminating between vertical reflections of the same object than between horizontal reflections. (Crudely, they are better at telling up from down than left from right). If, during training, they are rewarded for attacking the correct object rather than just indicating it in a nonhostile manner, then their learning rate improves too.

J. Z. Young has done several experiments to determine the effect on octopus vision of removal of the vertical lobe of its brain. But this is straying too far from goldfish.

SEX AND SMELL

Partridge, Liley and Stacey (1976) investigated the role of the sense of smell in mating behavior of the goldfish. The following (probably fictitious) dialogue summarizes their results:

1st Psychologist: "I say, I say, I say. My goldfish has no nose."

2nd Psychologist: "Your goldfish has no nose? Then how does it mate?"

1st Psychologist: "Infrequently."

What they did was to make male goldfish unable to smell either temporarily (by "occlusion of the nares," i.e., bunging up their noses) or permanently (by cutting their olfactory nerves). In either case the fish showed a marked decrease in sexual behavior.

Later, male fish which could smell were tested in a Y-shaped maze, one branch of which contained a sample of the ovarian fluid of an ovulated female. Their preference for that branch indicated the presence of pheromones which the goldfish could smell in the fluid. This all confirms that male fish discriminated between receptive and nonreceptive females by chemical cues.

The scientists spurned caviar in their quest for fish pheromones.

THE GOLDFISH FIGHTS BACK

Dekker and Groen (1956) give the case study of a patient who reported that the sight of a goldfish caused her to suffer asthmatic attacks. The good doctors, in their wisdom, ordered a goldfish bowl to be brought in. On its arrival, the woman at once had a severe attack of asthma. The goldfish itself, however, was exonerated when it was discovered that a plastic goldfish in a bowl also brought on an asthma attack in the woman. Finally, an empty goldfish bowl was found to cause just as bad a reaction.

Eventually the whole thing was traced back to an unhappy childhood experience which the woman had with a goldfish. Being unjustly accused of responsibility for asthma attacks may help explain why the goldfish in Shishimi (1985) were found to have latent inhibitions.

REFERENCES

Dekker, E. and Groen, J. (1956). "Reproducible psychogenic attacks of asthma." *J. Psychosomatic Research*, 1, 58.

Herter, K. (1930). "Weitere Dressurversuche an Fischen." *Z. vergl. Physiol.*, 11, 730–48.

Ingle, D. J. (1985). "The goldfish as a retinex animal." *Science*, 227, 651–5.

Partridge, B. L., Liley, N. R. and Stacey, N. E. (1976). "The role of pheromones in the sexual behaviour of the goldfish." *Animal Behaviour*, 24, 291–9.

Rowley, J. B. (1934). "Discrimination limens of pattern and size in the goldfish, *Carassius auratus*." *Genet. Psychol. Monogr.*, 15, 245–302.

Shashoua, V. E. (1968). "RNA changes in goldfish brain during learning." *Nature*, 217, 238–40.

Shishimi, A. (1985). "Latent inhibition experiments with goldfish *(Carassius auratus)*." *J. Comp. Psych.*, 99, 316–27.

Sunderland, N. S. (1957a). "Visual discrimination by octopus." *British J. Psychology*, 48, 55–71.

Sunderland, N. S. (1957b). "Visual discrimination of orientation and shape by octopus." *Nature*, 179, 11–13.

Sunderland, N. S. (1958a). "Visual discrimination of shape by octopus: squares and triangles." *Quarterly J. Experimental Psychology*, 1958, 452–8.

Sunderland, N. S. (1958b). "Visual discrimination of the orientation of rectangles by octopus *Vulgaris Lamarck*." *J. Comp. and Physiol. Psychol.*, 51, 452–8.

Sunderland, N. S. (1959a). "Visual discrimination of shape by octopus: circles and squares, and circles and triangles." *Quarterly J. Experimental Psychology*, 11, 24–32.

Sunderland, N. S. (1959b). "A test of a theory of shape discrimination in octopus: squares and triangles." *J. Comp. and Physiol. Psychol.*, 52.

Sunderland, N. S. (1960). ''Visual discrimination of orientation by octopus: mirror images.'' *British J. Psychology*, 51, 1.

Timms, A. M. (1976). ''The effects of vision on the general locomotor behaviour of the goldfish, *Carassius auratus*.'' *Animal Behaviour*, 24, 376–80.

The fish was simply not interested in learning to fly.

Chapter Three

Synchronized Drowning

The science of synchronized drowning predates the sport of synchronized swimming by at least ninety years, though apparently only dogs were allowed, in general, to participate, apart from the occasional rabbit, cat or guinea pig.

The Royal Medical and Chirurgical Society of London formed the first large-scale synchronized dog-drowning experiments as part of their investigations into the subject of "suspended animation." Their object was to discover techniques of bringing back life to creatures which had stopped breathing.

At the first meeting of the Committee it was resolved to pursue the inquiry:

By means of experiments upon living animals.

By means of experiments upon the dead human body.

Two subcommittees were forthwith appointed for these purposes.

The first experiments were concerned simply with the effects of depriving an animal of air. The subcommittee hit on an effective way of doing this: a glass tube was inserted into the animal's windpipe, then a tightly fitting cork was used to plug the tube. A long pin was also stuck into the animal in such a manner that it twitched whenever the heart beat.

Experiment 1—A full-grown healthy dog was suddenly de-

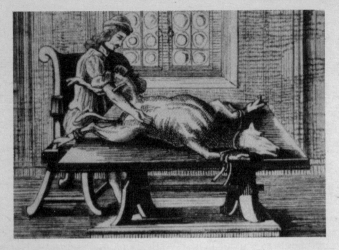

This method of blood transfusion can kill both animal and researcher
simultaneously.

*prived of air by plugging the tube. Its first struggle occurred
in 25 sec.; its first respiratory effort was not recorded, its
last took place at 4 min. 40 sec., and its last heart beat at
6 min. 40 sec., or exactly 2 min. after the last respiratory
effort.*

In experiment 2, another dog lasted 7 minutes, finally dying 3½ minutes after its last breathing attempt. The collie in
experiment 3 set a new record at 7 min. 45 sec.

After nine experiments, they had five dead dogs, three
dead rabbits and a dead cat. Dogs seemed to last a little
longer than rabbits. *As regards the cat, as only one experiment of this kind was performed, no average can be drawn.*
(Pussycat—you gave your life in vain!)

Having discovered how long it takes to kill a dog, the next
step was to determine for how long an animal can be de-

"No! Don't take the guinea pig too!"

prived of air, yet still recover. A few dead dogs later, they decided it was about four minutes. Then the experiments began to get fancy:

Exp. 18—A guinea pig was held so that its nose was immersed in mercury, the animal being upside down, and the nose inserted sufficiently deep in the mercury to prevent the possibility of getting any air . . .

Exp. 19—A terrier was deprived of air by plunging its head into liquid plaster of Paris, the object being to see, through the whiteness of the plaster, whether any of the fluid obtained access to the lungs.

The preliminary work done, the stage was set for the introduction of synchronized drowning.

Exp. 20—A medium-sized dog was fastened to a board, and submerged in a large bath. It was removed in 4 minutes, but although the heart went on acting for 4½ minutes longer, it neither gasped nor moved.

Two more dogs were used up in experiments 21 and 22, so they decided to shorten the drowning time until one survived. Experiment 25 brought the first dog survivor—after a minute's drowning. Four more died in establishing that 1½ minutes is too long. They wondered if the animals' struggling contributed to their demise; they wondered if cold water on the body hastened its end. One dead cat and six dogs later, they decided these factors were not important.

It was experiment 38 which brought the first true case of synchronized drowning:

Two dogs of the same type were fastened to the same plank and submerged at the same moment, but one of them had previously had its windpipe plugged in the usual way, and the other had not. At 2 min. they were taken out together; the one that had been plugged at once recovered, the other died.

They tried chloroforming dogs before drowning them. They tried various methods of artificial respiration on drowned dogs; but artificial respiration was not perfected in those days. The score for this phase of the experiments: 22 more dead dogs, 2 more dead guinea pigs, 9 dog survivors (but the dog which had recovered after drowning in experiment 72 did not survive experiment 76).

Total scores: 50 dogs, 2 rabbits, 2 cats and 3 guinea pigs

killed at the first attempt, 20 dogs survived their first experiment, but two of those succumbed later. Only one dog survived two trips to the research laboratories.

In the work of the second subcommittee, who used dead
bodies for their subjects, no harm was done to anyone. Most
of their subjects, already suffering from rigor mortis and early
phases of decomposition would probably have been sur-
prised to find that anyone was still interested in them.

Despite the efforts of the first subcommittee, the dog species continued to flourish and provide experimental subjects
for later generations of scientists. Some dogs, perhaps with
vestigial race memories of the horrors on their ancestors,
took to drink. (See the section on Alcohol.) Later canines
even began to fight back.

In a paper entitled "Human Deaths Induced by Dog
Bites," William G. Winkler analysed the eleven fatal attacks made by dogs on humans in America in the two
years 1974–5. His conclusion was to recommend that behavioral scientists should take up the research in order to determine the etiology of the attacks. That means he would like
to know why dogs kill humans. Nobody ever suggested that
behavioral scientists ought to determine the etiology of the
50 fatal attacks on dogs by humans in 1862.

Apart from alcoholism and homicide, other dogs have
shown a more basic way of registering their disapproval.
Jason, Zolik and Matese in 1979 evaluated two behavioral
strategies designed to increase the number of dog owners
who pick up their dogs' droppings. At the start of research,
they discovered that only 5% of owners stopped to scoop.
The first strategy, using signs to encourage the collection of
dog feces, had little effect, but instructions and modeling
raised the pick-up rate to 80%.

"No, Cynthia," explained the professor, "Drowning dogs is a man's job."

One basic inadequacy of the report was the omission of any data to discriminate between "good" owners and "bad" owners (in the sense of feces collection). Results have been obtained, however, to differentiate between the personalities of cat-owners and dog-owners. As a result of tests administered to 223 pet-lovers, we now know the following:

All pet-lovers are high on autonomy, but none so high as male cat-lovers.

Male pet-lovers in general, and dog-lovers in particular, have high scores on dominance, but female cat-lovers are low on dominance.

Male dog-lovers tend to be aggressive, a feature notably lacking in female cat- or-dog lovers.

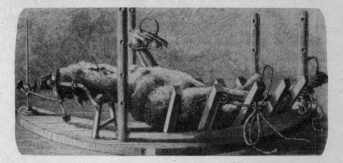

Irrational Fears in the Dog.

According to the authors of this study, the demonstrated differences in owner personality should facilitate matching pets and people to maximize the physical and psychosocial therapeutic benefits of pet ownership. (I think this means that it will help people decide whether they want a cat or a dog.)

So far, the dogs have not had much fun in these experiments. In order to redress the balance, we must turn to the *Veterinary Record* for August 1972, where there is a paper entitled: ''The Erect Dog Penis: A Paradox of Flexible Rigidity.''

''Twelve live dogs were observed and palpated alone and during coitus and a further eighteen fresh or embalmed dogs were dissected . . .''

Well at least the first dozen had some fun.

One dog problem remains unsolved, however. A paper in the *Canadian Journal of Psychology* in 1952 was entitled ''Irrational Fears in the Dog.'' When, as we have seen, a dog is liable to have a plug inserted into its windpipe, or to be drowned, or to have its sexual activity interrupted by a scientific palpator, how can any fear be described as irrational?

REFERENCES

Frank and Frank (1982). "Information processing in wolves and dogs." *Proc. 3rd Int. Theriological Congress.*

Gantt, W. H. (1952). "Effect of alcohol on the sexual reflexes of normal and neurotic male dogs." *Psychosom. Med.*, 14, 174–81.

Jason, L. A., Zolik, E. S. and Matese, F. J. (1979). "Prompting dog owners to pick up dog droppings." *Amer. J. Community Psychol.*, 7, 339–51.

Kalmur, H. (1955). "The Discrimination by the nose of the dog of individual human odours and in particular of the odours of twins." *Brit. J. Anim. Behav.*, 3, 25–31.

Kidd, A. H. and Kidd, R. M. (1980). "Personality characteristics and preferences in pet ownership." *Psychological Reports*, 46, 939–49.

Melzack, R. (1952). "Irrational fears in the dog." *Canadian J. Psychol.*, 6, 141–7.

Petrova, M. K. (1945). "Effect of chronic use of alcohol on the higher nervous activity of dogs." *Trud. fiziol. lab. Pavlov.*

Williams, C. J. B., Brown-Sequard, C. E., Harley, G., Kirkes, W. S., Hyde Salter, H., Sanderson, J. B., Savory, W. S., and Sieveking, E. H. (1862). "Report of the Committee appointed by the Royal Medical and Chirurgical Society to investigate the subject of Suspended Animation." *Trans. Roy. Med. & Chirurg. Soc. Lond.*, 27, 449–92.

Winkler, W. G. (1977). "Human deaths induced by dog bites, United States 1974–75." *Public Health Reports*, 92, 425–9.

Part Two

Natural Sciences

There are far too many natural sciences, so I have chosen to concentrate upon three of them: chickens, worms and spiders. These do, indeed, appear to be of major importance, with relevances outside their own limited domains, both natural and unnatural.

Apart from the splendid *Worm Runner's Digest* the history of scientific periodicals has had little to boast in the field of worms. Spiders have the *Journal of Arachnology* and the *Bulletin of the British Arachnological Society*, but the periodical literature on chickens more than remedies the deficiencies in the other two areas. The following is only a brief selection:

Broilers, which changed its name in 1961 to
Chickens, later (in 1965) to become known as
Chicken and Egg.

On a slightly more general theme we have:

Poultry Abstracts   *Poultry Farmer*
Poultry Forum   *Poultry Science*

Poultry World
Poultry Chronicle
Poultry Review
Poultry Business
International Journal
of Poultry Science

British Poultry Science
Poultry Fancier
Poultry Journal
World's Poultry Science
Journal

Chapter Four

Chickens

The science of chickens dates back more than a century. A seminal paper in 1873 by O. Spalding on "Instinct" was the egg from which generations of chicken experiments were hatched. In order to discover how much instinct played a part in the early behavior of chicks, he hatched nine eggs in a flannel bag. A day or two after hatching, he placed each chick in turn three meters from a box containing a hen and other chicks. They all ran to the hen, but not before they had stopped to think about it for a minute or so.

So far, so good. But maybe sight or sound of the hen contributed to this behavior. Had Spalding thought of this? Of course he had. As part of his experimental design, three chicks had had their heads covered with hoods from the earliest moment of hatching, and three more chicks had had earplugs fitted. When hoods and plugs were removed, the chickens behaved just like their all-hearing, all-seeing brothers and sisters. The blindfolded chicks did, however, appear to be afraid of worms.

Interestingly, chicks kept blindfolded for up to three days showed no fear of humans, but similar treatment for four days left them terrified of people. (Particularly psychologists, if they had any sense.)

Spalding's epoch-making advances in Chicken Science still left many questions unanswered, but later researchers have done their best to fill the gaps in our knowledge. The first natural question which springs to mind concerns the instinct of the young chick to respond to its mother. What happens, you may well be asking yourself, if we hack out the chick's brain? Will this affect it in any way?

N. E. Collias finally answered this important question in 1950: *Decerebrated chicks will not move towards a clucking or retreating object*. Though he did discover that leaving the basal portions of the cerebral hemispheres intact did not interfere with the chick's social responses.

The hen-chick relationship has been explored at great length. G. H. Bruckner in 1933 established the importance of sound rather than sight in mutual recognition between hen and chick. A sitting hen was taken away from her chicks in the dark and replaced by another broody hen. The chicks found their own mother. He then put two hens with their chicks together in one room, then removed one hen and disguised it with bandages. *When she was returned to the room, she noisily tried to divest herself of the bandages.* Despite the disguise, her chicks came to her at once. Perhaps dark glasses and a false mustache would have been a better disguise, but for some unaccountable reason this latter experiment was never performed.

Here we must launch into a brief digression concerning the usefulness of disguise as an aid to research in bird behavior. The false mustache, so oddly neglected by Bruckner in his chicken research, proved invaluable to G. K. Noble in 1936 in his experiments on courtship of the flicker. (This type of American woodpecker also travels under the name *Colaptes auratus luteus*.) When Noble attached a false male mustache onto the face of a wild female flicker, he found that her mate attacked her just as though she were a rival

Singular Execution of the Countess of Salisbury in 1541.

The Countess of Salisbury showed reluctance to be decerebrated at her execution in 1541.

The psychologist observed the chickens closely by cleverly disguising
himself as a watering can.

male. A violent reaction, perhaps, but one can understand
the bird's attitude towards a woman who suddenly sprouts a
mustache.

And these were not the only female birds to have been
disguised as males. A year before wrecking the domestic
bliss of a pair of woodpeckers, Noble (this time in collabo-
ration with Vogt) had been experimenting with a male yellowthroat (*Geothlyptis trichas*). When a stuffed female of the
same species was introduced into its cage, the yellowthroat
copulated with it. Then a black mask was placed on the face
of the stuffed bird to simulate male plumage. This proved
too much for the yellowthroat, who now attacked the object
of his previous affection. The researchers drew conclusions
only about the sex-recognition abilities of the experimental

animal. They did not comment upon their luck in finding a necrophiliac bird to begin with, nor on their disappointment that this ornitho-pervert was not also turned on by a bit of transvestism.

Meanwhile, back in the relatively straight world of new-laid eggs, we have not finished with the work of G. H. Bruckner. Working without the help of disguises, he also discovered that a lost chick gives distress calls which bring the hen quickly to its rescue. But if the chick is covered with a bell jar, preventing any sound from escaping, the hen will not react even if she can see the chick.

He concludes that the hen reacts only to the chick's call. This seems rather a simplistic explanation. We might conjecture that the presence of a bell jar enables the hen to reason that scientists are in the vicinity, and therefore the chick is, in fact, perfectly safe. Unless they cut its brain out, swathe it in bandages or adorn it with an unwanted moustache.

These experiments have added two important facets of experimental design to the repertoire of the dedicated researcher: surgery and disguise. For decerebration is not the only potential hazard for the experimental chicken; neither are bandages and moustaches alone among the resources of the wardrobe department.

De-beaking and artificial combs have both been employed in research into pecking orders. The whole social hierarchy of chickens is determined by real or mock fights which establish the pecking order. E. B. Hale in 1948 discovered not only that de-beaking does not interfere with the establishment of a pecking order, but that beak removal actually increases the frequency of pecking.

Students of form in these pecking contests would naturally be interested in factors which might be useful in predicting the outcome. Absence of molt and comb size have been established as useful tips in looking for a potential winner, but we had to wait for A. M. Guhl and L. L. Ortman in 1953 to establish the value of a cosmetic comb. They boosted the egos of several rather wimpish pullets by fitting them with impressive artificial combs. Thus adorned, the birds won more battles than before and were generally avoided by other pullets. Not surprising really; avant-garde style setters are often shunned by society until their innovations catch on.

Passing quickly over research into the visual perception abilities of chickens (the usual stuff—ability to discriminate between circles and triangles, or between rice grains of different colors and all that sort of thing), we must mention only the important result of Kroh and Scholl who, in 1926, taught a fowl to take grains of cereal from blue circles and to leave those on red triangles. When offered grains on red circles and blue triangles, the bird without hesitation took from the blue triangles. We now move on to mating behavior.

The courtship behavior of the brown leghorn cock was definitively analyzed by Wood-Gush in 1954. Three pens of hens were observed in their reactions to five brown leghorn cocks, and their "voluntary crouches" recorded. In all cases, the cocks were found to have accomplished their seductions by acting their way through a repertoire of nine actions: waltzing, tid-bitting (pecking, scratching and food calls), wing-flapping, cornering, feather-ruffling, tail-wagging, head-shaking, bill-wiping and preening. After that lot, the hens finally got the message and the research moves on to the next stage.

C. W. Upp was apparently the first, in 1928, to report that the maximum number of copulations among chickens takes place in the afternoon. This observation appears to have fas-

. . . The courtship behavior of the brown leghorn cock was definitively
analyzed by Wood-Gush in 1954 . . .

cinated a succession of researchers into watching the poor
cluckers going about their business, taking notes as they
watched. In 1937, A. G. Skard allowed one cock to copulate
in the mornings only for three days, before releasing it with
his hens for the entire time. Apparently the cock acquired a
taste for the new regime, copulating more in the morning for
a couple of days thereafter. On his most active day, the cock
was observed to copulate 53 times.

There is a problem in the interpretation of such a result
because it is hard to be sure whether the matings were all
successful. *Accordingly, in 1942, Parker, McKenzie and
Kempster designed and fitted a semen collector to their cocks.*
They reported that 14% of apparently normal matings resulted in no semen in the collector. Further, the semen content of the collector was consistently lower than that obtained

by manual massage. (Apparently such deviant behavior with a chicken was perfectly legal, even in 1942.) This whole piece of research has been criticized on the grounds that the cocks were only released for 15-minute periods and may consequently have been overexcited. Later researchers have been careful not to let their cocks get overexcited.

Long and Godfrey in 1952 discovered that *temperature had no effect on a cock's mating behavior, except when its comb and wattles were injured by freezing.* Well, mating can't be much fun if your wattles are frozen.

Intelligence and language in chickens have also attracted much interest. If you give a chicken a line of grain at which to peck, with alternate grains stuck down, it will quickly learn only to peck the free ones. And given the choice between two small collections of grain, they will generally prefer the larger offering. But it is in their language that chickens show greatest signs of intelligence.

A recent piece of research (Marler, Dufty and Pickert, 1986) tells us a great deal about the manner and content of the average chicken mealtime conversation. A certain type of clucking has been identified as a "food call." When a cock is in the presence of a hen, and there is food about, his food calls increase in rate and number according to his preference for the food. The hen is more likely to approach a male uttering such food calls than to saunter up to a silent male. She is also more likely to approach when his calls indicate the availability of good food than when merely average nosh is on offer.

This behavior is very similar to that observed in humans. Females are more likely to respond to males who invite them to dinner than to silent males, and a positive response becomes progressively more likely as the suggested restaurant improves. Just as the human male might lie about the food on offer, the chicken also indulges in mendacious behavior to get his bird: in the presence of a strange female, the cock has been heard uttering enthusiastic food calls, even when no food is about.

If he has food, and there is no female in the vicinity, his food calls decrease. If, however, there is another male around, they decrease still further. (Humans have also been known to lie about what's in the fridge when an uninvited caller of the wrong gender pays a visit.)

Few of the above chicken-related phenomena have direct applications, so we end this brief survey with two more observations of more relevance to industry. The first, not surprisingly, is connected, like so much other research, with alcohol.

In 1967, a researcher traveling in Romania observed a peasant farmer soaking his chicken feed in alcohol. The farmer had noticed that intoxicated cocks would become broody and relieve the hens from their job of sitting on the eggs. Getting the cocks drunk therefore left the hens free for egg production during the hatching season.

The researcher naturally conducted experiments on his return home to confirm this behavior in drunken chickens. His positive results appeared in a paper entitled ''Maternal behavior in the domestic cock under the influence of alcohol'' which was published in 1967.

Less successful was a research project conducted at the Atmospheric Science Research Center in New York in 1975. In an attempt to devise a simple way to estimate the wind speed of tornados, chickens were placed in a wind tunnel. The idea was to establish the wind force needed to pluck a chicken. If this could be done, it would provide immediate

CHICKENS FOR USE AND BEAUTY.

Silver (laced) Wyandottes.

information about any tornado which left a trail of plucked chickens in its wake.

Unfortunately, the research indicated that the force required to remove feathers from their follicles varied in a complicated and unpredictable way. The chicken's condition and environment could also make a considerable difference. The conclusion therefore was that *chicken plucking is of doubtful value as an index of tornado wind velocity.*

REFERENCES

Bruckner, G. H. (1933). "Untersuchungen zur Tiersoziologie, insbesondere zur Auflösung der Familie." *Z. Psychol.*, 28, 1–105.

Collias, N. E. (1950). "Some basic psychological and neural mechanisms of social behaviour in chicks." *Anat. Rec.*, 108, 552.

Graham, W. R. (1932). "Can we learn anything from a free choice of feeds as expressed by chickens?" *Poult. Sci.*, 11, 365–6.

Guhl, A. M. (1950). "Heterosexual dominance and mating behaviour in chickens." *Behaviour*, 2, 106–119.

Guhl, A. M. (1951) "Measurable differences in mating behaviour of cocks." *Poult. Sci.*, 30, 687–93.

Guhl, A. M. and Ortman, L. L. (1953). "Visual patterns in the recognition of individuals among chickens." *Condor*, 55, 287–98.

Hale, E. B. (1948). "Observations on the social behaviour of hens following de-beaking." *Poult. Sci.*, 27, 591–2.

Kroh, O. and Scholl R. (1926). "Vergleichende Untersuchungen zur Psychologie der optischen Wahrnehmungsvorgänge. II: Über die Teilinhaltliche Beachtung von Form beim Haushuhn." *Z. Psychol.*, 100, 260–73.

Marler, P., Dufty, A. and Pickert, R. (1986). "Vocal communication in the domestic chicken." *Rockefeller Univ. Res. Center.*

Noble, G. K. (1936). "Courtship and sexual selection of the flicker (*Colaptes auratus luteus*)." *Auk*, 53, 269–82.

Noble, G. K. and Vogt, W. (1935). "An experimental study of sex recognition in birds." *Auk*, 52, 278–86.

Parker, J. E., McKenzie, F. F. and Kempster, H. L. (1940).

"Observations on the sexual behaviour of New Hampshire males." *Poult. Sci.*, 19, 191–7.

Spalding, D. (1873). "Instinct." *Macmillan's Magazine*, 27, 282–93.

Vonnegut, B. (1975). "Chicken plucking as measure of tornado wind speed." *Atmos. Sci. Res. Ctr. State Univ. of New York, Albany.*

Wood-Gush, D. G. M. (1954). "The courtship of the brown leghorn cock." *Brit. J. Anim. Behav.*, 2, 95–102.

Wood-Gush, D. G. M. (1955). "The behaviour of the domestic chicken: a review of the literature." *Brit. J. Anim. Behav.*, 3, 81–110.

METHOD OF OBTAINING SKELE-TONS OF MICE, FROGS, &c.

If a mouse or a frog, or other like animal, be placed in an ant-hill, it will be devoured in a few days to the bones and ligaments. Hence we are furnished with a method of obtaining skeletons of those animals, exquisitely beautiful, and perfect, and far surpassing any thing that can be executed by artificial anatomy. The subject for this purpose is to be enclosed in a wooden box, and properly distended, to prevent the parts from collapsing or being crushed together by the earth. The box is to be perforated with a number of holes, through which the insects will presently find their way.

                                                        J. R.

Chapter Five

Worms

Some of the most apparently bizarre scientific experiments in recent years have featured the flatworm. For about 10 years beginning around 1960, experimental psychologists spent much time and effort giving worms electric shocks, slicing worms lengthwise, mincing worms and feeding them to other worms, and all to establish what would be the effects on the memory of the worm.

The whole subject deserves an introduction if only to establish the theoretical framework over which a multitude of worms were soon to be crawling.

The deep underlying question is one of the nature of long-term memory and whether learning is accompanied by biological changes at a molecular level. The theory would maintain, roughly, that learning something corresponds to a re-wiring of the connections between brain neurons. Then it needs the synthesis of new molecules of RNA to spread the good word.

Enter the flatworm (or planarian to its friends), the lowest organism to possess the same synaptic type of nervous system as the human. If the above theory is correct, the worm should be able to learn in the same re-wiring manner. So all we need to do is take a worm, teach it something, give some of its RNA to another worm and see if any of the learned information is also transferred.

So much for the theoretical basis, let's go and play with worms.

The first man to try to train worms was Van Oye in 1920. His technique was to teach the planarians to find food lowered into their bowls on the end of a wire. In order that the worms should be properly motivated, he starved them before the experiments. His results, claiming to show that worms were indeed capable of learning, were generally ignored. Two reasons might be conjectured: firstly, he was forty years ahead of his time since nobody else was interested in worms in 1920; secondly, his results were published in Dutch.

The next worm-trainers came along in 1953, when James V. McConnell and Robert Thompson began their research at the University of Texas. They taught worms to cringe.

Each worm was put in turn into a trough full of pond water. As the worm was crawling along the length of the trough, a light was turned on for a few seconds. With the light still on, an electric shock was then passed through the water. The shock caused the worm to contract, and the object of the whole design was to establish whether the worm could be conditioned to respond to the light by contracting, without waiting for the electric shock. According to McConnell and Thompson, the results established that worms can indeed learn.

As an experimental animal, the flatworm has a marvellous attribute: you can chop it into pieces and wait for each piece to regenerate into a complete new worm. This important fact led to phase two of the Great Worm Experiment. As McConnell explained: "It was while we were running our first experiment that Thompson and I wondered aloud, feeling rather foolish as we did so, what would happen if we con-

Comforting the worm after electric shocks.

ditioned a flatworm, then cut it in two and let both halves regenerate. Which half would retain the memory?''

Sadly, Thompson received his doctorate before the question could be answered. He moved to another university and exchanged worms for rats. But McConnell, who had already displayed that rare virtue in a researcher—the ability to feel foolish—was to persevere in a worm-ridden career. With a unique mixture of experimental zeal, insight and humor, he was to head the Planaria Research Group at the University of Michigan, where he was also founder and editor of the *Worm Runner's Digest*. Described as an "Informal Journal of Comparative Psychology," the Digest is perhaps the most delightful scientific publication ever conceived.

Back on the research, we left McConnell wondering what happened to a worm's memory if you chopped it in half. He had a chance to find out in 1956. The experimental design was as follows:

Train a group of worms, taking note of the time they take to learn their lesson; cut each worm in half; store head and tail sections separately; wait 4 weeks for regeneration to take place; retrain regenerated worms and compare the retraining time with the original learning time to determine whether any memory of the early lessons was retained.

For comparison purposes, two further groups of worms (control groups) had to be included. The first control group comprised worms which were excluded from the original training, but were chopped in half anyway, just to see if regeneration itself affected learning ability. The second control group were luckier: they were trained, not bisected, left for four weeks then retrained. Their role was to show how much forgetfulness played a part in the need to retrain the regenerated sample.

The results of the experiment showed not only that the regenerated heads seemed to retain knowledge, but that the tail sections also grew back into educated worms. It seemed that memory was somehow stored throughout the body of the flatworm.

The next stage was to start with an uneducated worm, cut it in half, teach the head something, then let it regenerate, cut it in half again and finally allow the new tail half to grow back into a complete worm. This final animal thus contains nothing of the bit which had the original lessons. They called it a "total regenerate." And they found that total regenerates also show retention of learning.

By now worm-training was becoming popular. Other researchers were training worms to find their way through simple mazes and seeing if the maze-learning also survived regeneration. One novel piece of research added another dimension to the regeneration theme: worms' heads were split down the middle and each half was allowed to regenerate. The resulting organism, a two-headed worm, was then trained along with one-headed worms. The conclusion was that it learned more quickly. Two heads are better than one.

The next stage was to see if it was possible to transfer learning from one worm to another. Some years were spent trying to graft trained heads onto the untrained tails of other worms. Then they tried grinding up trained worms and injecting them into uneducated worms. Finally came the breakthrough. Under suitable circumstances, worms can be persuaded to eat other worms. Such cannibalistic behavior is too good an opportunity to waste. *"We conditioned a number of worms, chopped them into small pieces and hand-fed the pieces to trained cannibals."* (Of course, some untrained worms were also fed to untrained cannibals to act as a control group.)

And the diet of worms seemed to work. Minced worm apparently gave the recipient some of the knowledge its meal had previously learned. The answer to the question: "Is knowledge edible?" appeared to be "Yes." Food for thought indeed.

What began with flatworms naturally spread to other creatures. Rats' brains were injected with extracts prepared from educated rats. Chicks' brains were injected with essence of bright-chick brain. Until about 1970, the chemical transfer of learning (especially in worms) was threatening to become mainstream experimental psychology. Then it all began to go out of fashion.

All the original conclusions began to be called into question. Had the researchers sufficiently taken into account the effects of the worms' slime trails? Was it really established that worms could learn anything at all? Did we really know what we meant by learning anyway?

Nowadays, the whole topic seems to have fallen under a very gray cloud. Those who decide these things have ruled that knowledge is not edible and the days of the great wormrunners appear to be over. At the psychology laboratories of the world, minced worm is off the menu, for the time being anyway.

REFERENCES

Bennett, E. and Calvin, M. (1964). "Failure to train planarians reliably." *Neurosciences Research Program Bulletin*, 2, 3.
Hartrey, A. C., Keith-Lee, P. and Morton, W. D. (1964). "Pla-

Revenge of the nematodes.

naria: Memory transfer through cannibalism re-examined.''
Science, 146, 274.

McConnell, J. V., Jacobson, A. L. and Kimble, D. P. (1959).
''The effects of regeneration upon retention of a conditioned
response in the planarian.'' *J. Comp. physiol. psychol.*, 52,
1–5.

McConnell, J. V., Jacobson, R. and Humphries, B. M. (1961).
''The effects of ingestion of conditioned planaria on the response level of naive planaria.'' *Worm Runner's Digest*, 3,
41–5.

McConnell, J. V. (1962). ''Memory transfer through cannibalism in planarians.'' *J. Neuropsychiat. Suppl.*, 1, 3, 42.

McConnell, J. V. and Mpitsos, G. (1965). ''Effects of the
presence or absence of slime on classical conditioning on
planarians.'' *Amer. Zool.*, 5, 122.

Pickett, J. B. E., Jennings, L. B. and Wells, P. H. (1964).
''Influence of RNA and victim training on maze learning by
cannibal planarians.'' *Amer. Zool.*, 4, 411.

Riccio, D. and Corning, W. C. (1969). ''Slime and planarian
behavior.'' *Psychol. Rec.*, 19, 507.

Smith, S. J. (1963). ''An attempt to replicate the cannibalism
studies.'' *Worm Runner's Digest*, 5, 49–54.

Van Oye, P. (1920). ''Over het geheugen bij fr flatwormen en
andere biologische waarnemingen dij deze dieren.'' *Natu-
urwet. Tijdschr.*, 2, 1.

Ziegler, R. A. (1963). ''Is knowledge edible?'' *Worm Runner's
Digest*, 5, 55–7.

Chapter Six

Spiders

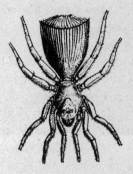

A Neotropical spider (*Chorizops loricatus*).

Not many people know much about spiders, but a few dedicated researchers know a great deal indeed. Whether spiders are courting, copulating, fighting, spinning webs, taking drugs, or any combination of the above, someone is probably watching them and taking notes.

AGGRESSION

A great deal of social behavior in spiders is governed at least to some extent by their aggressive and occasionally cannibalistic habits toward one another. Approaches between spiders, whether of the same or opposite sexes, have therefore to be tentative. One of their principal modes of communication is through vibrations along the radii of a web. (The radii, incidentally, are much stronger than the spiral threads. The spiral threads are much stickier than the radii.)

The mechanism controlling how spiders make friends with other spiders has been conjecturally attributed to a pheromone that inhibits biting. To test this theory, B. Krafft in 1970 (*Biologica Gabonica*, 4, 307–69) performed experiments with various lures planted on a web. The lures were made to vibrate at a frequency of around 100 Hz in order to attract the interest of the spider occupying the web. If the lure was a cricket or a ball of elder pith, the spider would approach and bite it. If the lure was another spider, the occupant would tolerate its presence, whether the lure was alive or dead.

For this part of the experiment, dead spiders had been killed with carbon dioxide, in order not to change their smell. The importance of smell was demonstrated by offering a lure of a spider washed in a mixture of alcohol and ether. Such "clean" spiders were attacked and bitten. (It might be observed that humans who smell of alcohol and ether are also often treated badly by their fellows.) Crickets washed in alcohol and ether were bitten more often than similarly treated spiders.

Next, he tried balls of ether pith made to smell like spiders by sprinkling ground-up spiders over them. These were often bitten, though if the grindings were from spider abdomens, they were less likely to be attacked.

All these findings are consistent with the theory that spiders like the smell of something in other spiders' abdomens.

MATING

The courtship of spiders is fascinating, because they apparently only like to mate with their own species, but sometimes have difficulty recognizing whether another spider meets this description.

First, we must mention a result of Jackson (1981), who seems to have spent a good deal of time watching the mating behavior of the jumping spider *Phiddipus johnsoni*. He observed that females kill the males in approximately 1% of their interactions, which is about the same rate at which males kill females. When they are not killing each other, the female is most likely to mate with a male who dances during the courtship ritual. This trend is even more pronounced when the females are non-virgins. It is most regrettable that comparable statistics are not available for humans. One might conjecture that the attitudinal difference to dancing between spider virgins and non-virgins would be found to be reversed in humans. But the research has yet to be done.

G. W. Uetz and G. E. Stratton, in Witt and Rovner (1982), report several studies on the role of various forms of communication during courtship. By putting spiders in insulated bell jars or plastic bubbles, they were able to test for responses to sight, sound or smell of other spiders. Males, apparently, get turned on by the silk of females (which contains pheromones), but they need movement before they will initiate mating.

This was confirmed with forced mating experiments where females were anesthetized with CO_2. When presented with a non-moving female, the male would not approach to copulate. However, if the female was moved, even slightly, the male would orient to her and approach.

This confirmed that visual or chemical stimuli alone are not sufficient for mating to be initiated by the male. It should be stressed that these experiments were done in Cincinnati, where being an accessory to the rape of a spider is no crime.

In the courtship experiments, they had noticed that females always rejected the advances of males from other spider species, yet there are species with identical genitalia, such as *Schizocosa rovneri* and *Schizocosa ocreata* which, though physically capable of it, do not interbreed.

"We then performed a series of forced copulations to test for interfertility." After a period of courtship by a male of the wrong species, females of each type were anesthetized with CO_2, then placed in front of the male and slowly moved forward with front legs extended. The randy little arachnids needed no further temptation, but promptly mounted the unresisting females. *When females emerged from under the influence of the CO_2, the male was already mounted, and they responded as if in a "normal" mating.*

The offspring were great fun too, with the males switching happily between courtship patterns of both species.

COMMUNICATION

We have already mentioned the topic of spider communication by vibrations. Usually such conversations take place along the radii of the web, but other media are also possible. The best work in this field has been done by Rovner and Barth (1981) who showed that spiders can send each other messages along the leaves of banana plants. By playing ran-

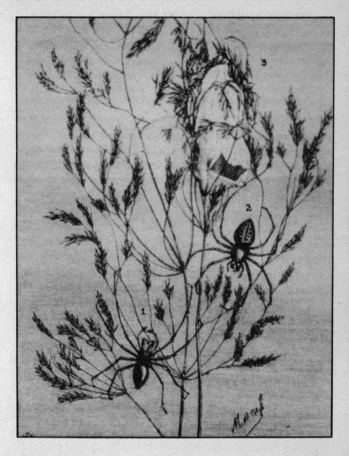

Male and female spiders (1) and (2) prepare to enter the mating cocoon
(3) for a bit of privacy.

dom noise out of loudspeakers, they prevented the spiders
from communicating through sound. Then they recorded the
vibrations in the leaves made by a male and a female spider.

The relationship between vibrations made by the male and those made by the female demonstrated that they were indeed "talking" to one another.

SPIDERWEBS

The first important thing to note is that scientists always refer to them as "spiderwebs," never spider's (or spiders') webs. Having got our terminology correct, we can proceed to the work of Peter Witt, the best web-watcher in the business.

In 1954, Witt recorded the effect on the webs of giving drugged food to spiders. The webs of *Zilla-x-notata* spiders were disturbed, particularly when benzedrine, marihuana and scopolamine were put into the spider's food. He noted the specific disturbances characteristic of each drug and began a remarkable study into the identification of a wide range of drugs through their effects on spiderwebs.

Reed and Witt (1968) looked at the effects of two sedative drugs on web geometry. Phenobarbital was found to have stronger effects than diazepam. (It's the other way round for humans, but humans don't spin webs.) The sedatives also have the effect of making the spiders lazy and imprecise in their movements.

Reed, Witt and Jones (1965) had already found another way to disturb web formation: they cut some of the spider's legs off. *"Spiderwebs were analyzed with the aid of a computer before and after the removal of a single first leg, or the first two ipsilateral legs."* The legless spiders were found to produce webs with significantly fewer radii, fewer spiral turns, less spiral area and shorter overall thread length. No differences were found between the effect of chopping off

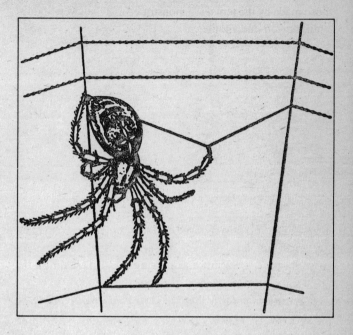

A spider spiding.

one right leg or one left leg. (Spiders appear therefore not to be right- or left-legged.)

The first leg is known to be used for measuring as well as walking. These results showed that the second leg can partly, but not totally substitute for that function. Painting the eyes of a spider with black lacquer, incidentally, does not have any effect on its web-building.

The effect of hallucinogenic drugs on spider webs has been the most exciting area in this field. After discovering the types of web disturbance caused by a wide range of different

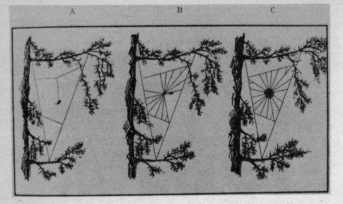

A step-by-step guide to web-spinning for spiders.

drugs, Witt and others developed the ''spider test'' to identify small amounts of such substances. Spiders were successfully used to identify scopolamine and mescalin in the urine samples of psychiatric patients.

The experimental technique is to concentrate the urine by various extraction processes into a small amount of solid, which is then dissolved in sugar water and fed to the spider. Then you wait for it to spin a web, measure the disturbances and compare them with the known effects of different drugs.

Having shown that it worked, the next stage was to test the urine of patients who were suffering from hallucinations, in order to determine whether the body was itself producing something similar to hallucinogens. Many spiders drank a lot of urine during these experiments, but the best results came not from urine but from blood.

N. A. Bercel (1959) fed the blood of schizophrenic patients to spiders. After putting the blood through a centri-

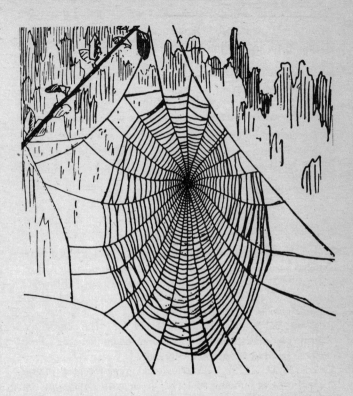

An eccentric web can indicate disturbance in the spider.

fuge, the resulting serum was put in the amputated abdomen
of a fly, which was then placed in a *Zilla-x-notata* web. The
spider ate the serum, and the effects of its web were noted.

The first effect noted was that intake of any serum always
reduced the frequency with which a spider spun webs. In
several cases there were also minor abnormalities in the web

formations, but the most striking results were seen in the frequency with which rudimentary webs, having just a few strands each, were produced. Such webs are often seen from spiders prior to molting. But here they were seen in 66.7% of cases in which spiders had drunk the blood of catatonic patients.

The next stage was to feed the bodies of molting spiders to normal spiders. The normal spiders were again observed to produce rudimentary webs as a result of the meal.

The conclusion is that there may be something similar in the blood of catatonic schizophrenics and the body fluids of molting spiders. Further research is clearly needed.

REFERENCES

Bercel, N. A. (1959). "The effect of schizophrenic blood on the behavior of spiders." In: *Neuro-psychopharmacology*, P. B. Bradley, P. Deniker, C. Radouco-Thomas (Eds.), Elsevier.

Boys, C. V. (1880). "The influence of a tuning fork on the garden spider." *Nature*, 23, 149.

Bristowe, W. S. and Locket, G. H. (1926). "The courtship of British lycosid spiders and its probable significance." *Proc. Zool. Soc.*, London, 1929, 309–58.

DeVoe, R. D. (1975). "Ultraviolet and green receptors in principal eyes of jumping spiders." *J. General Physiology*, 66, 193–207.

Forster, L. M. (1977). "Mating behaviour in *Trite auricoma*, a New Zealand jumping spider." *Peckhamia*, 1, 35–6.

Jackson, R. R. (1977a). "An analysis of alternative mating tactics of the jumping spider, *Phidippus johnsoni*." *J. Arachnol.*, 5, 185–230.

Jackson, R. R. (1977b). "Courtship versatility in the jumping spider, *Phidippus johnsoni*." *Animal Behavior*, 25, 953–7.

Jackson, R. R. (1977c). "Prey of the jumping spider, *Phidippus johnsoni*." *J. Arachnol.*, 5, 145–9.

The web of a sober spider.

Jackson, R. R. (1980). "The mating strategy of *Phidippus john-soni*: II. Sperm competition and the function of copulation." *J. Arachnol.*, 8, 217–40.

Jackson, R. R. (1981). "The relationship between reproductive security and intersexual selection in the jumping spider *Phidippus johnsoni*." *Evolution*, 35, 601–4.

Kaston, B. J. (1936). "The senses involved in the courtship of some vagabond spiders." *Ent. Amer.*, 16, 97–167.

Koomans, M. J., van der Ploeg, S. W. F. and Dijkstra, H. (1974). "Leg wave behavior of wolf spiders of the genus *Pardosa*." *Bull. British Arachn. Soc.* 3, 53–61.

Montgomery, T. H. (1903). "Studies on the habits of spiders, particularly those of the mating period." *Proc. Acad. Nat. Sci. Phil.*, 1, 59–149.

Pickard-Cambridge, F. O. (1881). "The spiders of Dorset, with an appendix containing short descriptions of those spiders not yet found in Dorsetshire, II." *Proc. Dorset. Nat. Hist.*, 237–625.

Reed, C. F. and Witt, P. N. (1968). "Progressive disturbance of spider web geometry caused by two sedative drugs." *Physiology and Behaviour*, 3, 119–34.

Reed, C. F., Witt, P. N. and Jones, R. L. (1965). "The measuring function of the first legs of *Araneus diadematus Cl.*" *Behaviour*, 25, 98–119.

Rovner, J. S., Higashi, G. A. and Foelix, R. F. (1973). "Maternal behaviour in wolf spiders: the role of abdominal hairs." *Science*, 182, 1153–5.

Rovner, J. S. and Barth, F. G. (1981). "Vibratory communication through living plants of a tropical wandering spider." *Science*, 214, 464–6.

Witt, P. N. (1954). "Spider webs and drugs." *Scientific American*, 191(6), 80–6.

Witt, P. N. (1956). "Die Wirkung von Substanzen auf den Netzbau der Spinne als biologischer Test." Springer, Berlin.

Witt, P. N. (1958). "The identification of small quantities of hallucinatory substances in body fluids with the spider test." In: *Psychopathology, A Source Book*. C. F. Reed, I. E. Alexander and S. S. Tomkins (Eds.), Harvard.

Witt, P. N. (1965). "Do we live in the best of all worlds? Spider webs suggest an answer." *Perspect. Biol. Med.*, 8, 475–87.

Witt, P. N. and Rovner, J. S. (1982). *Spider Communication*, Princeton.

Part Three

Social Sciences

The social sciences with which we shall be concerned here are those of principal interest to humankind: Sex, Courtship and Bodies, if not necessarily in that order. Although all of these have been around for some time, they have long been denied a proper scientific study. Now, however, we can be pleased that there is a lot of it going on, all properly documented.

Keeping up with the progress in such a diverse area is not always easy. It is further complicated by constant changes of names within disciplines. What used to be known as "Comparative and Physiological Psychology" later adopted the more esoteric title of "Animal Ethology" and now generally calls itself simply "Animal Behavior."

Furthermore, there are hundreds of journals of psychology and sociology and social psychology and clinical psychology and abnormal psychology in which to publish new research. For those who wish to specialize, the following can be recommended:

British Society for the Study of Sex Psychology (which ran from 1914–1933)

Journal of Sex Research

Advances in Sex Hormone Research

International Journal of Sexology (incorporating *Marriage Hygiene*)

Archives of Sexual Behaviour

British Journal of Sexual Medicine

Sexual and Marital Therapy

Studies in Sexual Politics

Sexual-Probleme (incorporating *Zeitschrift für Sexualwissenschaft*)

Journal of Reproduction and Fertility

International Journal of Fertility

Chapter Seven

Sex

(Owing to the highly complex and structured nature of the material in this section, it has been felt advisable to introduce a numerical classification system, in order to ease the reader's path through a formidable body of knowledge, and to dampen any feelings of excitability which this body might otherwise engender.)

7.0 HISTORICAL INTRODUCTION

Until recently the study of sex, like sex itself, was something which was only officially sanctioned to consenting adults in private. Comments on sexual behavior were made only by the medical profession, who were naturally concerned mainly with problems which they thought they could treat. Sir Astley Cooper's Surgical Lectures, published in *The Lancet* in 1824, were remarkably frank about the causes and cures of sexual malfunctions such as Premature Ejaculation:

Sometimes it is the result of debauchery, but most frequently it occurs in irritable and delicate young men; in such cases we have to support the constitution, by a generous diet and bark, giving at the same time opium to allay

The birds and the bees.

the irritability. In addition to which let the person stand over a large pan of cold water and dash it over the genitals two or three times in the day. Turpentine and rhubarb are sometimes given, but I am not sure that they do any good.

His comments on impotence are equally valid:

[Impotence] may sometimes be traced to a peculiar sluggishness of constitution, to a general torpor of the procreative system, on which the usual animal affinities exert no influence. To such a person a Venus might display her charms, and on such her son might exhaust his quiver, in vain . . . When consulted on this point before marriage, you should ask, if they have any development of sexual power in the morning, and if they have, depend on it they will not be deficient in energy in the after part of the day. But if otherwise, advise them by no means to marry.

For the treatment of married men suffering from impotence, Sir Astley could offer no better recommendation than three to four days' abstinence and a placebo.

Only later did medical men begin to take interest in the woman's viewpoint. Dr. E. Cushing, a Boston physician, was one of the first to comment on the female orgasm. Admittedly he thought of it as a disease, which could only be cured by "orgasm's destruction," but his scientific approach was still a small step forward. Modern views, however, do not approve of the genital surgery that he practiced on female patients "suffering" from orgasm.*

With this brief historical overview of the subject in mind, we may now move on to more modern ideas about sex. In such a diverse and exciting field of research, the subject areas are many and highly ramified. For ease of reference, we divide our material into the main categories: Sex Differences,

---

*Further discussion may be found in Gluckman, 1963: "The Role of the Sexes in Wiko Circumcision Ceremonies." On the other hand, it may not.

Castration, Coitus (including interruptus), Stimulation and Repression, Homosexuality and Deviation.

7.1 SEX DIFFERENCES

7.1.1 Humans

In the pre-empirical days, when scientific beliefs were often based on the way things ought to be, rather than on perceived evidence, Aristotle claimed that women had fewer teeth than men. As no less a man than Bertrand Russell pointed out: ''Aristotle could have avoided the mistake . . . by the simple device of asking Mrs. Aristotle to open her mouth.''

Nowadays, any scientific pronouncements on sex differences are based only on the most painstakingly collected data, as in the following extract which explains why men make better engineers:

The capacity of the penis and testicles to move and retract presents the boy with a particular challenge in the development of the body image; this may contribute to his interest in machinery, physics and the like.

The boy's better spatial sense relates to the greater use he makes of space in motor activity; the ability the boy has to perceive his sexual organ may also contribute to a better representation of space and to his better skill and greater interest in experimental sciences and mathematics. (from: Bertrand Cramer, ''Sex Differences in Early Childhood.'' In: *Child Psychiatry and Human Development*, 1971, 1, 133–51).

Commenting on this observation, the *Journal of Irreproducible Results* in 1985 concluded that women would presumably make better speleologists.

7.1.2 Chaffinches

We have already referred to the effect of artificial combs on pullets (*see*: Chickens, chap. 4), which raises the natural question: What happens if female chaffinches have their underparts dyed red? P. Marler (1955) supplied the answer: it improves their position in the social hierarchy. The underparts of a sample of female chaffinches were dyed red, in imitation of males of the same species. These chaffinches were then found to win the great majority of aggressive encounters with normal (undyed) females, and accordingly dominated them in the pecking order.

Interestingly, this result remained true when the experimental chaffinches were all females reared by hand, never having been allowed to set eyes on a male. In fights with males, the findings become still more intriguing. Red-dyed

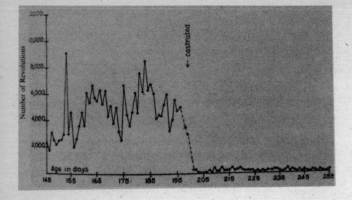

Spontaneous running activity of a male rat showing the effect of castration.

females will still, in general, be dominated by males, but not if the females have been separated from all male company for four to five weeks.

In other words, in the chaffinch world, dressing like a male and talking only to other women can make a bird very butch indeed.

7.2 CASTRATION

7.2.1 Mice

How does castration affect the mating habits and abilities of the mouse? Is the post-castration effect in any way controlled by the genetic structure of the animal? The answers to these crucial questions are to be found in McGill and Tucker's (1964) excellent research work into the sex drive of castrated mice.

72 male mice from 3 different genetic strains helped with

the experiment. So did 252 female mice. Each day, for 42 consecutive days, 36 females were "brought to behavioral estrus" (made randy) by hormone injections. Each male mouse was placed in the testing chamber, given time to settle down, then given a female mouse. He was allowed 5 to 10 minutes in which to begin mating. If, within that time, he showed no interest, then the female was replaced. If he refused 3 females, he was scored "negative" for that day. In order to score "positive," mating to ejaculation was demanded. If the male began mating, but withdrew prior to ejaculation, he was given another 40 minutes to resume action.

Each male thus had a theoretical maximum score of 42 (one for each day of testing) on the ejaculation scale. After those six merry weeks, half the males were castrated. Three days later, the experiments were resumed for all the mice except the two which had died as a result of the operation. Daily testing then continued until ejaculations ceased. The results are summarized in tables 1 and 2 below.

Table 1   *Sexual performance of intact male mice*

Strain number	Number of Ejaculators	Average numbers of ejaculations per ejaculator	Average day of first ejaculation
1 (24 mice)	10	2	17
2 (24 mice)	22	15	3
3 (24 mice)	24	15	2

Table 2 *Sexual performance of mice after castration*

Strain number	Number of castrates	Number of pre-operative ejaculators	Number of post-operative ejaculators	Total number of post-op ejaculations
1	11	4	0	10
2	11	10	3	3
3	12	12	9	42

Strains 1 and 2 were purebred genetic stock; Strain 3 were hybrids. As can be seen from these tables, Strain 1 was a rather wimpish, sexless lot, with only 10 ejaculators and even they were unimpressive. Strain 2 almost kept pace with Strain 3 during the first phase of the experiments, but it was after castration that Strain 3 finally demonstrated their true class. As table 1 shows, of ten Strain 2 mice which had scored before the operation, only three had any fun after it—and they only managed once each. But the hybrid Strain 3 went on for another 4 weeks, with 9 out of 12 continuing to perform.

What this study confirmed was the principle of "hybrid vigour." As an interesting by-product, *the results also indicated that "fast-recovery" males were capable of more ejaculations over an extended time period than were "slow-recovery" males*.

7.2.2 Cats, Dogs, Guinea Pigs and Rats

Rosenblatt and Aronson (1958a), Rosenblatt and Aronson (1958b), Stone (1927), Beach and Levinson (1950), Cooper and Aronson (1958) and others have shown that *the sexual behavior of experienced male cats and dogs persists much longer after castration than that of guinea pigs and rats*.

7.2.3   Hamsters and Starlings

They too have laid down their gonads in the quest for knowledge. See Beach and Parker (1949) and Davis (1957).

7.3   COITUS

7.3.1 Non-interruptus

Several authors have commented upon damage received to the compound eye of some female dragonflies while mating. The maximum injuries reported involved denting of perhaps 50 ommatidia in each compound eye. This is close to the highest amount of head damage sustainable without leading to death. Apparently it is the male epiproct which does the damage.

Perhaps the female dragonflies would do better to experiment with different mating positions, in order to keep their ommatidia out of the way of their lovers' epiprocts. According to Tricas and Le Feuver, who observed and photographed sharks mating off Hawaii in 1985, they copulated in "stationary parallel orientation," with their heads on the bottom (the sea bottom, presumably) and bodies angled upwards at approximately 45° into the water. *Pair contact was maintained by the male's left clasper anchored in the female's vent and her left pectoral fin held tightly in his mouth.* And she had no trouble from any epiprocts.

7.3.2   Interruptus

According to Makkink's classic work "Die Kopulation der Brandente," displacement bathing has been observed regularly in the shelduck when copulation was interrupted for some reason. He does not mention that humans similarly have been known to take a bath if interrupted when copulat-

Preparing to take a measurement of the shark's copulating angle.

ing. But perhaps that had not been properly researched in 1931.

Rats, however, being more dedicated copulators, are not so easily interrupted. A series of papers in 1964 examined "The Effect of Auditory Stimulation on Reproduction." It was discovered that loud noises can distract, or at least reduce the fertility of, copulating rats. The fourth paper in the series, entitled "Experiments on Deaf Rats," made a significant addition to this knowledge: ". . . The experiments show that auditory stimuli during the copulation period do not cause a decrease in fertility in deafened rats in contrast to normal animals."

Loud noises do not distract deaf rats.

Displacement bathing in ducks disturbed while copulating.

7.4 STIMULATION AND REPRESSION

7.4.1 Goats

An experiment which combined elements of sexual exhibitionism, voyeurism and bondage was conducted on goats
in 1984. Nine male dairy goats were individually exposed to
a single, restrained estrous female goat. Tests were conducted under four different conditions:

W: Another male watching the goat being tested;
S: The tested goat having just watched another male
     court and copulate with the female;
SW: Both the above;
C: None of the above.

Results showed that each form of stimulation, S, W and SW, enhanced the sexual performance of the goat under test. The female goat's opinion is not recorded.

7.4.2 Turkeys

Precocious sexual behavior can be induced in the young turkey (poult) by means of injections of androgen. This is therefore a good way of examining innate sexual reactions in experimental animals which have had no previous sexual experience.

In order to discover what turns turkeys on, Schein and Hale (1959) took turkey poults between 5 and 8 weeks of age. 3 different stimulus objects were used as potential sexual releasers; a poult head, mounted on a stick; a headless poult body (stuffed); and the hand of an experimenter.

Given the choice among these objects, no poult showed preference for the headless body. "Fully organized copulatory movements" were recorded in at least some cases in response to the other stimuli. Birds with early social experience of other turkeys tended to prefer the head, but birds which had been reared in isolation liked the hand best of all.

The whole experimental design might be criticized on the grounds that the experimenter's hand, unlike the poult head, was not cut off and mounted on a stick. Perhaps this will be rectified in later research.

7.4.3 Ruffled Grouse and Crow

The effects of fear and aggression on the sexual performance of birds have been investigated by Allen (1954). His results show that whereas fear suppresses male sexual behavior, it is aggression which has a sexually inhibiting effect on female crows and ruffled grouse. (Whether it was fear or aggression which ruffled the grouse in the first place is not recorded.)

7.4.4 Mice

It has been reported that in encounters with females, cannabis decreases the sexual behavior of male mice. Gay mice are presumably unaffected.

7.5 HOMOSEXUALITY AND DEVIATION

7.5.1 Mice, Pigs and Dutchmen

Researchers at the Aegean University in Ankara, Turkey, in 1984 reported that disco music causes homosexuality in mice and may have the same effect on humans. They report that *"high-level noise, such as that frequently found in discos, causes homosexuality in mice and deafness among pigs."*

Oddly, they offer no explanation of why the mice were resistant to deafness or how the pigs managed to maintain their sexual identities.

Further information on homosexuality may be found in Van Emde (1967): *The Position of Homosexuals in Holland*.

7.5.2 Monkeys

A detailed study (Mason, 1960) on the early sexual behavior of monkeys showed the profound effects of an unhappy childhood. The subjects were two groups of adolescent rhesus monkeys.

The Restricted Group comprised three males and three females, all born in the laboratory, separated from their mothers before they were a month old, then housed in individual cages with sight and sound of other monkeys, but with no opportunities for physical contact.

The Feral Group was three males and three females, all

1. Quietude.

2. Sadness

3. Laughter

4. Weeping

5. Anger

6. Excitement

How to spot a chimp with an unhappy childhood.

captured in the field, having grown up in the wild. At the start of experiments, all the monkeys were aged 28–29 months.

Monkeys were tested in pairs, each test session lasting 3 minutes. Their activities were monitored, with episodes of play or sexual activity recorded. Monkeys of the Restricted Group were found to play more than the Feral Group. But the Feral males "showed more mounting and thrusting and had sexual episodes of substantially longer duration." Furthermore, males in the Restricted Group never clasped their partners' legs with their feet during mounting and would frequently assume inappropriate postures and body orientation. The Feral females were also observed to flex their legs as the partner mounted, while intent gazing and rapid lip movements prior to mounting were also characteristic of both males and females in that group. These behaviors were never observed among the Restricted Group.

A second experiment was done which showed that the sexual responsiveness of the Restricted males increased strikingly when they were tested with experienced females instead of the young innocents of their own group. In fact their mounting average rose from 0.2 to 2.44 per session. But they still tended sometimes to adopt inappropriate orientation (e.g., trying to mount from the side).

Finally, in case anybody wants to try their own experiments in this area, we should draw your attention to an invaluable research tool mentioned in the *Journal of Behaviour Research Methods and Instrumentation* in 1971:

An instrument that may be of interest to some researchers or behavior modifiers is accessory kit PM-1P. It allows one to *hear* changes in penile expansion for an additional $30.

REFERENCES

Abel, G. G. and Blanchard, E. B. (1976). "The measurement and generation of sexual arousal in male sexual deviates." In: M. Hersen, R. Eisler and P. M. Miller (Eds.), *Progress in Behaviour Modification, Vol 2*, Academic Press, NY.

Allan, A. A. (1954). "Sex rhythm in the ruffled grouse (*Bonasa Umbellus*) and other birds." *Auk*, 51, 180–99.

Beach, F. A. and Levinson, G. (1950). "Effects of androgen on the glans penis and mating behavior of castrated male rats." *J. Experimental Zoology*, 114, 159–71.

Beach, F. A. and Parker, R. S. (1949). "Effects of castration and subsequent androgen administration upon mating behaviour in the male hamster (*cricetus auratus*)." *Endocrinology*, 45, 211–21.

Cooper, M. and Aronson, L. R. (1958). "The effect of adrenalectomy on the sexual behaviour of castrated male cats." *Anat. Rec.*, 131, 544.

Davis, D. E. (1957). "Aggressive behaviour in castrated starlings." *Anat. Rec.*, 128, 537.

Dunkle, S. W. (1984). "Head damage due to mating in *Ophiogomphus* dragonflies." *Not. Odonatol.*, 2.

Gluckman, M. (1963). "The role of the sexes in Wiko circumcision ceremonies." In: *Social Structure*, Meyer Fortes (Ed.). Russell & Russell, New York.

Hale, E. B. (1955). "Defects in sexual behaviour as factors affecting fertility in turkeys." *Poult. Sci.*, 34, 1059–67.

Keiser, S. (1952). "Body ego during orgasm." *Psychoanalytic Quarterly*, 21, 153–66.

McGill, T. E. and Tucker, G. R. (1964). "Genotype and sex drive in intact and in castrated male mice." *Science*, 145, 514–15.

Makkink, G. F. (1931). "Die Kopulation der Brandente (*Tadorna tadorna L.*)." *Ardea*, 20, 18–22.

Marler, P. (1955). "Studies of fighting in chaffinches. (2) The effect on dominance relations of disguising females as males."

Mason, W. A. (1960). "The effect of social restriction on the behaviour of rhesus monkeys." *J. Comp. and Physiol. Psychology*, 53, 582–9.

Price, F. O., Smith, V. M. and Katz, L. S. (1984). "Sexual stimulation of male dairy goats." *Applied Animal Behavioural Sci.*, 13.

Rosenblatt, J. and Aronson, L. R. (1958a). "The influence of experience on the behavioural effects of androgen in prepuberally castrated male cats." *J. Animal Behaviour*, 6, 171–82.

Rosenblatt, J. and Aronson, L. R. (1958b). "The decline of sexual behaviour in male cats after castration with special reference to the role of prior sexual experience." *Behaviour*, 12, 285–338.

Schein, M. W. and Hale, E. B. (1957). "The head as stimulus for orientation and arousal of sexual behaviour of male turkeys." *Anat. Rec.*, 128, 617–18.

Schein, M. W. and Hale, E. B. (1959). "The effect of early sexual experience on male sexual behaviour of androgen injected turkeys." *Animal Behaviour*, 7, 189–200.

Stone, C. P. (1927). "The retention of copulatory ability in male rats following castration." *J. Comp. Psychology*, 7, 369–87.

Van Emde, B. C. (1967). "The position of homosexuals in Holland." *Z. Psychosom. Med.*, 13, 55–63.

Chapter Eight

Courtship

Browsing through the December 1982 issue of the *National Geographic Magazine*, one might come across a description by a dedicated researcher who spent most of a day watching lions mating. They were observed to copulate, he tells us, 23 times in 5 hours and 20 minutes; and on 22 of these 23 times, it was at the instigation of the lioness.

I only mention this because it seems to be a typical example of what research is all about. The good researcher in this and allied fields must combine voyeurism with good note-taking abilities, curiosity with prurience.

You should already be wondering what interpretation to put on those prodigious leonine feats. How long had the researcher waited before those 5 hours and 20 minutes? Might he in fact have arrived late and missed the whole story? Or did he leave early, thinking that the lions had finished for the day, when in fact they were just taking a rest? And which of the 23 copulations did the male initiate? If you are asking yourself questions like these, you too may qualify for a research grant.

Whether it is lions, humans, butterflies, newts, sharks, rats, sparrows or any other living creatures, you can be sure that someone is studying their sexual habits. From the first moments of courtship, through mate selection, mating, orgasm and infidelity, the researcher will be there, monitoring every stage of the process in order to report to the eagerly awaiting world.

Sometimes, the science is simply one of observation. When Fred J. Alsop III saw a great crested flycatcher copulating with an immature eastern bluebird, he wrote it up for the *Annals of Applied Biology*. Any immature eastern bluebirds reading that journal will now know to watch out. When two entomologists at the University of Western Australia saw a male beetle, *Julodimorpha bakewelli*, trying to copulate with a beer bottle, they realized at once that the world had to be told.

Such discoveries are purely serendipitous, of course. A true researcher cannot just sit around all day hoping to spot some interesting copulation to write home about. So much of the work has to be laboratory based, testing theories of courtship. Some typically interesting recent discoveries have concerned mate selection in butterflies.

Recent evidence implies that male butterflies are limited in the number of ejaculations they may achieve in a lifetime. This means that they cannot afford to screw around non-reproductively. Since the reproductive value of female butterflies decreases with age, *it would be better evolutionary strategy for male butterflies to court young virgins than to waste their time on old mated females*.

Armed with this hypothesis, Wiklund and Forsberg (1986) devised their experiments to test it. Twenty-five females were bred in captivity to ensure that they retained their virginity. On reaching sexual maturity, they were released and followed, with the experimenters making detailed observations on any courtship attempts by males. In fact, 20 of the randy little girl butterflies mated with the first male they met. Three of the other 5 had their seduction interrupted by another male and the affair ended with the males flying in circles round each other.

The crucial data might have been more substantial had the virgins been a little less eager, but there were still apparently enough cases of males being rejected for conclusions to be drawn. When the courtships were examined in detail, it was found that a male butterfly will court an unreceptive virgin for approximately 60 seconds before giving up. But if the same male is courting an experienced female, he will take no for an answer after only 3 seconds.

The researchers deduced that the males' mating strategy is in line with evolutionary requirements. On the other hand, they might equally have deduced that old, experienced females are better at saying whatever is the butterfly equivalent of "piss off, sonny." (It is believed that human males also spend more time trying to seduce virgin females, though their motives may be less than evolutionary. Probably some research is already being done on this important topic.)

For those with deeper interest in the courtship rituals of the butterfly, some excellent work was done by Rutowski and Schaefer (1984), who took motion pictures of successful and unsuccessful courtships. In order to avoid having to rush around following butterflies with their cameras, the experimenters tethered the females (virgin females, of course—why settle for less than the best?). Their observations include an account of a previously undescribed wing-clap display by the male, during which he was often seen to catch the female's antenna between his own wings.

There is no suggestion in their paper that the males attracted to this particular experiment may have been sexually perverted butterflies with a bondage fetish. Anyone who has worked with humans in this field will know that tethered virgin females do tend to evoke unusual behavior on the part of free-flying males. Why should butterflies be any different?

One cannot be sure in these experiments that it is virginity which is so appealing to the males. Research on newts has shown that novelty, rather than inexperience, is what makes one newt sexually attractive to another. Verrell (1985) placed male newts in the presence of 4 potential mates. Most males in such circumstances were observed to engage in either 1 or

2 courtships. Their choice of partner was determined by their own previous experiences with the females on offer. *Male newts preferred novel females as mates, seldom courting previous partners.*

This has rather sad implications. The conclusion cannot be escaped that courting newts rarely, if ever, live up to each other's fantasies. Sparrows, however, perhaps lacking the erotic imagination of the newt, seem to prefer a monogamous existence. The reasons for sparrow fidelity are discussed by Greenlaw and Post (1985) in their research paper on the "Evolution of Monogamy in Seaside Sparrows."

Their task was to establish the beneficial nature of sparrow monogamy. In order to do so, it was necessary to trace the behavior of "experimentally widowed female" ("we used male-removal experiments . . ."). Such sad females were found to be able to rear about two-thirds as many young sparrows as two-parent sparrow families. It was concluded that normal family life is a good thing for young sparrows. The role of female-female aggression on monogamous behavior was also discussed, but more research was considered necessary in that area. And just to show that the birds were capable of it, *the researchers succeed in inducing experimental bigamy in New York seaside sparrows.* Perhaps in New York the sparrows are more open-minded.

Interestingly, it has also been discovered that experimentally prolonged sexual activity in female sparrows delays the termination of reproductive activity in their untreated mates.

Pied and collared flycatchers do not, according to Alatalo, Gustafsson, and Lundberg, have the same marital inhibitions as sparrows. In their discussion on "The High Frequency of Cuckoldry in Pied and Collared Flycatchers," they establish that 24% of broods involve multiple paternity. *By observa-*

Cleverly concealed behind a tree, the psychologist spied on unfaithful birds.

*tions of coloring and measurements of foot length, they con-
clude that the most likely cuckolder is the neighboring male.*
The high frequency of cuckoldry is attributed to the polyter-
ritorial behavior of the males. That means it's because they
fly around a lot.

Since the sparrow survey and the flycatcher report reveal
different patterns of family life, we must turn to rats once
again for an Animal Model for Infidelity in Man. This piece
of research from Ohio State University was designed to show
that familiarity, while not necessarily breeding contempt,
does little to enhance sexual attraction.

Rats were housed alone, or in pairs, or with a tennis ball,
for 10 days. There followed 10 more days of tests to establish
the degree of attraction each rat felt to tennis balls and to

other rats. *On the whole it was found that rats were more attracted to other rats than to tennis balls.* But housing a rat with either another rat or a tennis ball resulted in reduced attention to that object, but not to the other. In other words, if you live with a rat for long enough, you may begin to appreciate the finer points of tennis balls. And, of course, cohabiting with a tennis ball loses some of its glamor too after the initial thrill has worn off.

Rats, incidentally, would probably defeat the lions which introduced this chapter in any competition of sexual stamina—at least in the sprint events. Bermant (1961) devised an experiment in which female rats were conditioned to press a lever for a male to be introduced into their box. After copulating with the male, it was found that the female would press the lever again within 20 seconds, and would continue to do so for at least 5 consecutive copulations.

We have strayed some way from the topic of fidelity, but we have, thanks to the randy rat, introduced the concept of female sexual initiative. These two areas were brought together in a 1984 study on "Males' Response to Female Sexual Initiative in Committed Relationships."

"Recent research studies," reports the author, "indicate that males' attitudes toward female sexual initiation are positive." This study was intended to investigate precisely how males responded. Accordingly, 48 married or cohabiting heterosexual couples were divided into three experimental groups:

Group One: The females were instructed to initiate sex through direct verbal means.

Group Two: The females were instructed to initiate sex through non-verbal means.

Group Three: No instructions were given.

. . . all males responded positively to their female partners' sexual
initiatives . . .

Records were kept and questionnaires administered. The
results demonstrated that all males responded positively to
their female partners' sexual initiatives. Furthermore, high
levels of male satisfaction were recorded following female
initiation.

A less successful sexual initiative was reported in *Science
News* in December 1985, providing a novel variation on the
"Not tonight I've got a headache" theme. A man in Georgia
wore a nitrate patch on his chest in order to control heart
pain. An unfortunate side effect of this treatment was that it
gave him headaches. As an experiment, he moved the patch
onto his thigh. The headaches cleared up. Then, whether by
accident or design is not stated, he rubbed a used nitrate
patch on his penis. The effect was an unaccustomed level of

sexual arousal. He accordingly had sex with his wife. Several minutes later she complained of a colossal headache. The wife, clearly no dedicated research scientist, strongly discouraged further experiments.

This experience led to two discoveries: the ability of topical nitrates to induce vasodilation; and their ability to be absorbed through the membranes of the vaginal wall. For once, however, the authors expressed doubt that further research would be done in this area.

At this stage, we should mention a totally unrelated case study reported in the *Journal of the American Medical Association* in 1972. Entitled "Paroxysmal Sneezing Following Orgasm," it was exactly that (in a male). No physiological explanation was advanced, but it's a wise precaution to keep a box of paper handkerchiefs by the bed just in case.

Another wise precaution might be contraception. In 1976 Dr. T. Healey (*Science*, 93, 477) conjectured that contraception was playing its role in the spread of venereal disease in Scandinavia. The incidence of gonorrhoea had declined in Sweden, but not in Denmark. Dr. Healey noted that while the Swedes have a simple word "kondom," the Danish equivalent is "sangerskabsforebyggende middel," and hence the Danes buy fewer of them.

He does not, however, give the comparative sales figures for Coca-Cola in the two countries. It was left to three scientists from the Harvard Medical School to test the spermicidal properties of the soft drink, after reports that the Coca-Cola douche was a widely used technique in developing countries.

According to Peel and Potts (*Textbook of Contraceptive Practice*, 1st Edition, C.U.P. 1969, p. 149) the effectiveness of Coca-Cola as a spermicidal agent is due to its acidic pH.

"Not tonight dear, I've run out of Coca-Cola."

The Harvard study, comparing 4 different formulations of the drink, strongly suggests that some component of the secret formula must also be contributing.

The design of the experiment was to add sperm specimens (from a healthy donor, at 37°C) to test tubes containing sam-

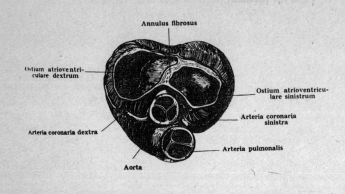

Annulus fibrosus

Ostium atrioventricu-
lare dextrum

Ostium atrioventricu-
lare sinistrum

Arteria coronaria
sinistra

Arteria coronaria dextra

Arteria pulmonalis

Aorta

An affair of the heart.

ples of Coca-Cola. After a minute, a measure was taken of
the number of sperm still moving. The results are shown in
the table below.

Coke Brand	% Sperm Motility after 1 min.	pH of Coke
Old (Classic)	8.5	2.38
New Coke	41.6	2.37
New caffeine-free	16.6	2.25
Diet Coke	0.0	2.89

What the experimenters do not take into account, however, is whether sperm actually like Coke. Perhaps they drank
a lot of the diet Coke and slimmed themselves to death. The
apparently greater effectiveness of Classic Coke could be due
to fundamental traditionalist tastes of the sperm.

In any case, the Coca-Cola company appears unimpressed

by this research. An official said: "We do not promote Coca-Cola for medical purposes. It is a soft drink."

REFERENCES

Alatalo, Gustafsson, and Lundberg, (1984). "High frequency of cuckoldry in pied and collared flycatchers." *Dept. of Zool.*, Uppsala Univ.

Alsop, F. J. (1971). "Great crested flycatcher observed copulating with an immature eastern bluebird." *Annals of Applied Biology*

Bermant, G. (1961). "Response latencies to female rats during sexual intercourse." *Science*, 133, 1771.

Greenlaw, J. S. and Post, W. (1985). "Evolution of monogamy in seaside sparrows." *Animal Behaviour*, 33, 373–83.

Forand, A. Q. (1984). "Males' response to female sexual initiative in committed relationships." Ph.D. Thesis, Univ. of Georgia.

Gwynne, D. T. and Rentz (1983). "Beetles on the bottle—Male buprestids mistake stubbies for female (Coleoptera)." *J. Australian Entomol. Soc.*, 22.

Makkink, G. F. (1931). "Die Kopulation der Brandente (*Tadorna tadorna L.*)" *Ardea*, 20, 18–22.

Rutowski and Schafer, (1984). "Courtship behavior of the gulf fritillary (*agraulis vanillae*)." *J. Lepid. Soc.*, 38.

Tricas and Le Feuver (1985). "Mating in the reef white-tip shark." *Marine Biol.*, 84.

Umpierre, S. A., Hill, J. A. and Anderson, D. J. (1985). "The effect of 'coke' on sperm motility." *New England J. Medicine*, 313.

Verrell, P. A. (1985). "Female availability and multiple courtship in male red-spotted newts, *Notophthalmus viridescens*." *Behaviour*, 94.

Wiklund, C. and Forsberg, J. (1986). "Courtship and male discrimination between virgin and mated females in the orange tip butterfly *Anthocharis cardamines*." *Animal Behaviour*, 34, 328–32.

Chapter Nine

Bodies

Now here's one you can try at home. All you'll need is a blank sheet of paper and a pencil. Now pick up the pencil and draw a person on the paper.

Finished? Good. You have just completed the test known to psychologists as the Draw-a-Person test. We now come to the interpretation, which has been a matter of detailed research and controversy for two or more decades.

THE DRAW-A-PERSON TEST

The theory behind the interpretation of the Draw-a-Person test is that the picture drawn is in some ways a projection of the subject's own body and personality. The first thing to look at is the sex of the person drawn. Research has shown that young children predominantly (about 90%) draw a figure of their own sex. As they grow older, boys continue to draw male figures, but girls draw progressively fewer female figures until, at eighteen, about half their drawings are found to be male. With so many females acting deviantly, they become bad subjects for study, so several researchers have restricted their studies to male subjects.

Grams and Rinder (1958) tested the hypothesis that males who drew pictures of females were homosexual or effeminate. Their findings failed to confirm the hypothesis. Whitaker (1961), however, altered the instructions slightly. He asked his subjects to draw first one figure, then another of the opposite sex to the first, then a third of either sex. His results indicated that 93% of those whose first and third drawings were both female were considered effeminate or homosexual.

Several other studies concerning the sex of the figure drawn have produced inconclusive results. Armon (1960) found a weak correlation between homosexuality in women and the tendency to produce drawings of men. A. Davids and S. De Vault in 1960 considered the effects of pregnancy and childbirth on women's performance in the Draw-a-Person test. They report that pregnant women are more likely than non-

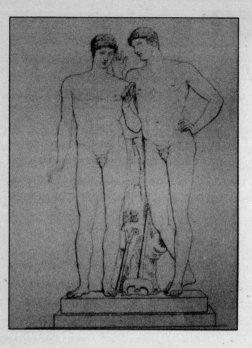

"My fig leaf's bigger than your fig leaf!"

pregnant women to produce drawings of females. Women who have had complications in delivering children are more likely to produce male drawings than women who have given birth without complications.

Several researchers have noted a tendency among male alcoholics to produce drawings of females. Kurtzberg, Cavior and Lipton (1966) reported that drug addicts also draw the opposite sex more frequently than nonaddicts.

Fischer (1961) noticed that if the figures drawn by male adolescents were nude, there was a greater chance they would

Foot-fetishists at play.

be female nudes. The depiction of sexual organs in the drawing is another matter which has been studied by a number of
researchers, but the results are inconclusive.

Having reached no satisfactory interpretation of the sex of
the figure, the next thing to look at is its size.

Several studies have reported a correlation between the size of the figure drawn and the self-esteem of the subject. Lakin (1960) hypothesized that institutionalized elderly people would draw smaller pictures (indicative of lower self-esteem) than non-institutionalized elderly people. His findings supported the hypothesis. A. McHugh (1963) hypothesized that Puerto Ricans and Blacks in the United States would also show a lack of self-esteem through the size of their drawings. The Puerto Ricans did; the Blacks didn't. V. Bennett in two studies between 1964 and 1966 found no significant relationship between size of drawing and self-esteem.

So the findings on size and sex are unconvincing (or at best inconsistent). Also whether the picture is in profile or full frontal, and the stance of the figure have been studied in relation to personality of the subject. The results suggest that no reliable conclusions can be drawn. A review of the considerable literature on this subject also shows no general agreement on the significance of other aspects of the picture including the following, all of which have been mentioned by one or more researchers: mouth, hair, neck, head, face, nose, arms, ears, earrings, teeth, eyes, eyelashes, hands, fingers, legs, feet, toes, heels, hips and buttocks.

On the subject of breasts, however, we should mention the result of Rierdan and Koff (1980) who showed that *girls in early adolescence are more likely than older adolescents to draw explicit breasts on their pictures of females*. Which brings us to our next topic.

BREASTS

Much valuable work has been done on breasts. According to an article in the *New Scientist* in 1964:

The breasts do form an important part of woman's biological equipment for courtship and it is a question not so much of morals as of tactics to consider at what stage in the proceedings they are to be deployed to the best advantage.

The paper by Kleinke and Staneski (1980) offers some pertinent observations on the whole subject. They carried out an experiment in order to determine what people see in breasts of different sizes. The subjects were 135 male and female undergraduates who were presented with photographs or descriptions of "Stimulus Persons" of varying bust sizes. The subjects were then asked to give written descriptions of the supposed personality attributes of the Stimulus Persons.

In fact, the researchers explain that the Stimulus Persons were "made to simulate small, medium and large bust sizes" for the photographs.

When the written descriptions were analyzed, it was found that the most favorable ratings were given significantly to women perceived as having medium-sized busts. On assessment of the photographs, large-busted ladies were evaluated as being relatively unintelligent, incompetent, immoral and immodest. Small-breasted ladies were rated most intelligent, competent, modest and moral.

Similar studies, asking for descriptions of the personality attributes of male silhouettes have shown that endomorphs (short and fat) are generally considered least likely to succeed, most likely to drink a lot, and least desirable as a friend, while mesomorphs (athletic and muscular) are considered the most natural leaders, least likely to smoke or drink, least likely to have a nervous breakdown, but most aggressive. Finally, the tall, thin ectomorph is marked down as a heavy smoker and drinker, and most likely to have a nervous breakdown before the age of thirty.

BODY IMAGE

All the above studies were concerned with subjects' drawing or their impressions of other people's bodies. Potentially far more revealing, however, is a person's attitude to his or her own body. The Body-Cathexis (B-C) scale gives the subject an opportunity to express feelings about various parts of his or her own body. 40 bodily items are listed and the subject invited to rate each of them on a five-point scale:

1 Have strong positive feelings.
2 Have moderate positive feelings.
3 Have no feeling one way or the other.
4 Have moderate negative feelings.
5 Have strong negative feelings.

(If you want to try this yourself, the 40 parts of the body to think about are: hair, facial complexion, appetite, hands, body hair, nose, physical stamina, bowel function, muscular strength, waist, energy level, back, ears, chin, body build, profile, height, keenness of senses, tolerance of pain, shoulder width, arms, chest (or breasts), appearance of eyes, digestion, hips, resistance to disease, legs, appearance of teeth, sex drive, feet, sleep, voice, health, sex activities, knees, posture, face, weight, sex organs.)

Jourard and Secord (1955a, 1955b) investigated Body-Cathexis (defined as the degree of satisfaction with parts of the body) and its relation with general self-esteem. One of

their first findings was that responses on the B-C scale cor-
related with actual body measurements. On five important
measures (height, weight, shoulder width, chest, biceps), the
responses showed that males tended to be more satisfied the
bigger they were. (Evidently the researchers did not have the
opportunity to measure all the 40 items in their list for a full
comparison.)

The reverse trend, however, was found for females. Direct
measurements taken of 12 body parts (height, weight, bust,
waist, hips, thighs, calves, ankles, feet, nose length, shoulder width, neck length) showed a strong tendency for smaller
measurements to obtain better ratings on the B-C scale. The
few correlations which implied that "big is beautiful" all
pointed, once again, at the bust.

This result was confirmed when females were asked to
give estimates of what they supposed to be ideal body measurements. Once again, *the figures showed that women tended
to think that most of their bodily parts were a bit too large,
except for their breasts which were too small*. In fact, they
concluded that the average girl thinks that she is 2.94 lb
overweight, has a waist 1.18 in too big, hips which should
be reduced by 2.37 in and a bust measurement 0.69 in too
small.

Their findings indicate, incidentally, that the ideal woman
is 65.53 in tall, weighs 122.48 lb, and her vital statistics are
34.83–24.27–35.06.

The whole question of the relationship between self-esteem
and satisfaction with one's own body has aroused much debate. Several researchers have taken the overall Body-
Cathexis score as a meaningful measure of satisfaction with
one's body. Others have stressed the importance of taking

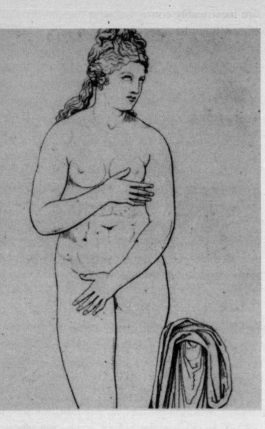

"Would that my tits were 0.69 inch bigger."

the items in the B-C scale independently. A detailed analysis by Mahoney and Finch (1976) revealed that things are not as simple as they might seem. They questioned the interpretations of earlier researchers who had isolated particular body-items as of high importance to self-esteem. Since body-parts are inextricably connected with one another, their B-C ratings will not be mutually independent. Only a sophisticated statistical analysis can determine the real contribution made by each item individually to self-esteem.

Their conclusions produced very different pictures of what is most important to males and females. The top bodily parts for each sex in their effect on self-esteem are as follows:

Males: 1. Voice 2. Chest circumference 3. Teeth
             4. Nose 5. Leg shape 6. Facial features
Females: 1. Overall physical attractiveness 2. Teeth 3. Hair
             color 4. Voice 5. Calves 6. Height 7. Hips

However dissatisfied women may claim to be about their bust measurements, it appears that when it comes to assessing their contribution to a lady's self-esteem the breasts hardly stick out at all.

REFERENCES

Armon, V. (1960). "Some personality variables in overt female homosexuality." *J. Projective Techniques*, 24, 292–309.

Berscheid, E., Walster, E. and Borhnstedt, G. (1973). "The happy American body: A survey report." *Psychology Today*, 7, 119–31.

Craddick, R. A. (1962). "Draw-a-Person characteristics of psychopathic prisoners and college students." *Perceptual and Motor Skills*, 15, 11–13.

Fischer, G. M. (1961). "Nudity in human figure drawings." *J. Clinical Psychology*, 17, 307–8.

Grams, A. and Rinder, L. (1958). "Signs of homosexuality in human figure drawings." *J. Consulting Psychology*, 22, 394.

. . . Women tended to think that most of their bodily parts were too
large . . .

Hansson, R. O. and Duffield, B. J. (1976). "Physical attractiveness and the attribution of epilepsy." *J. Social Psychology*, 99, 233–40.

Jourard, S. M. and Secord, P. F. (1955a). "Body-cathexis and
the ideal female figure." *J. Abnormal and Social Psychology*,
50, 243–6.

Jourard, S. M. and Secord, P. F. (1955b). "Body-cathexis and
personality." *British J. Psychology*, 46, 130–8.

Kleinke and Staneski (1980). "First impressions of female bust size." *J. Social Psychology*, 1980, 123–24.

Koppitz, E. (1966). "Emotional indicators on human figure drawings of shy and aggressive children." *J. Clinical Psychology*, 22, 466–9.

Kurtzberg, R. L., Cavior, N. and Lipton, D. S. (1966). "Sex drawn first and sex drawn larger by opiate addict and non-addict inmates on the Draw-a-Person test." *J. Projective Techniques*, 30, 55–8.

Lawton, M. and Sechrest, L. (1962). "Figure drawings by young boys from father-present and father-absent homes." *J. Clinical Psychology*, 18, 304–5.

Mahoney, E. R. and Finch, M. D. (1976). "Body-cathexis and self-esteem: A re-analysis of the differential contribution of specific body aspects." *J. Social Psychology*, 99, 251–8.

Rierdan, J. and Koff, E. (1980). "Representation of the female body by early and late adolescent girls." *J. Youth and Adolescence*, 9, 339–46.

Swenson, C. H., Jr. (1955). "Sexual differentiation on the Draw-a-Person test." *J. Clinical Psychology*, 11, 37–40.

Whitaker, L. (1961). "The use of an extended Draw-a-Person test to identify homosexual and effeminate men." *J. Consulting Psychology*, 25, 482–5.

Whitmyre, J. W. (1953). "The significance of artistic excellence in the judgment of adjustment inferred from human figure drawings." *J. Consulting Psychology*, 17, 421–2.

Part Four

Fine Arts

Lest anyone think that research into the fine arts is neglected compared with the sciences, let them browse through the following list of journals in our selected areas of Music and Parapsychology. (Sadly there seem to be no good journals on humor, unless you include *Animal Behavior Abstracts* which I always find a bundle of laughs.)

Music Now
Music Record
Music Student
Music Scene
Music in Middlesex
Folk Music Journal
World Music
Slovak Music
Acoustic Music
Soul Music
Black Music
Music in Worship
Detroit Studies in Music Bibliography

Chinese Music
Psychology of Music
Modern Music
Music and Poetry
Music and Letters
Music and Liturgy
Music and Man
English Church Music
Church Music
Church Music Review
Church Music of Today
Church Music Quarterly

Botanic Physician and Psychic Journal (which changed name
    to:
Botanic Annual and Psychic Journal
*Quarterly Journal of the International Institute of Psychic
    Investigations*
*Quarterly Transactions of the British College of Psychic Sci-
    ence*
Psychic Researcher and Spiritualist Gazette
Advances in Parapsychology Research
Christian Parapsychological Papers
Parapsychology Bulletin
Journal of Parapsychology   *Research in Parapsychol-*
Psychic Research Quar-   *ogy*
terly   *Christian Parapsychology*
Psychic Science   *Psychic Researcher*

Chapter Ten

Music

The effects of alcohol on musical ability have never been properly researched.

The subject of music research is too vast to condense into one short chapter. Composition, performance, appreciation, musicology, ethnomusicology, instruments, instrumentalists, songbirds and gibbon song have all been studied intensively. What follows is only a brief snatch of melody from the symphony of research into the major topics of interest.

MUSICAL APPRECIATION BY PIGEONS

It has been reported that playing Beatles songs underwater frightens sharks. Further, experiments in zoos have suggested that jazz appeals to cheetahs but not to monkeys, but the most reputable such research concerns pigeons. Porter and Neuringer (1984) investigated the ability of pigeons to discriminate between complex musical sequences. By rewarding birds for the correct identification of the composer of music played to them, *the experimenters taught pigeons to discriminate between one-minute excerpts of Bach flute music and Hindemith viola music*. Two pigeons managed more than 80% success after training on this task.

In a more complex task, the pigeons were required to generalize from short samples of a long piece of music. Excerpts from Stravinsky's *Rite of Spring* or a twenty-minute Bach organ piece were played to the birds after they had been trained on short extracts from the same works. They were slow to learn, but eventually four pigeons managed 70% success on the task, even when they were required to classify portions of the music they had never heard before.

Pigeons, of course, having no great aptitude as singers, probably prefer listening to performing. There is no indication in the above paper as to any preferences they might have expressed between Bach and Hindemith, or Bach and Stravinsky. It has, however, been reported that rats can be trained to prefer Mozart to Schoenberg. Our next topic deals with the bird as performer.

SONG STRUCTURES IN THE CANARY

Guettinger (1985) discusses the effects of domestication on the song structures of the canary. Here is a bird which for many generations has been reared as a house pet. Tamed and refined, its songs might be expected to reflect this domestication process. On analyzing and comparing the sound qualities of domestic and wild canaries, however, he found that their songs were remarkably similar (". . . the general acoustic morphology has remained astonishingly stable during the long process of domestication . . .") Only a few changes were detected in characteristics of some of the syllables. Rough syllables have been nearly eliminated, and short syllables have become far more frequent.

This must, however, all be viewed in the context of some more general work on canary songs by Dr. Fernando Nottebohm of the Field Research Center, Rockefeller Univ. N.Y. (quoted in *Strange Things*, by R. K. G. Temple, London 1983). Every winter, the canary loses 20% of its brain. The *pars caudale* vanishes almost completely, while more than three-quarters of the *nucleus robustus archistriatalis* also shrivels up. These are the parts of the brain which include the memory for song. The missing bits of the brain grow back in the spring, but the canary has to learn a new repertoire of songs.

Perhaps this helps to explain why canaries are not renowned for singing duets. If you and your partner are both going to forget the tunes every winter, it must make duetting difficult. Bornean gibbons, however, do sing duets according to Mitani (1985). He has observed that mated adult pairs engage in frequent bouts of interactive song duets. Since each pair occupies and forages within a specific area, it is conjectured that duets play a function in "intergroup spacing" (telling other gibbons to keep off their patch).

MUSICAL PERFORMANCE

If you want to improve the performance of musicians, recent research has established two ways to do it: you can give them drugs, or you can lie to them about the music they are playing.

The Russian psychologist L. L. Bochkaryov in 1975 connected contestants in an international music competition to equipment which would measure galvanic skin response, temperature and heart rate. These physiological measurements did not differentiate between successful and unsuccessful contestants on readings immediately before performance (though the unsuccessful looked anxious and reported feeling more nervous). During the performance, however, arousal levels were higher among the successful musicians.

Taking this one stage further, James, Griffith, Pearson and Newbury (1977) investigated the use of drugs to inhibit "stage fright" in musicians. When the sympathetic nervous system causes sweaty palms and tremor, these symptoms add to the anxiety of the performer who thus becomes even sweatier and more trembly. So an appropriate drug might be one that inhibits the action of the sympathetic nervous system. Oxyprenolol is one such drug (a so-called beta-adrenoceptor-blocker). So the researchers enlisted the services of 24 mu-

Science comes to the aid of the violinist who has trouble playing in tune.

sicians about to give a stressful performance, giving each at random either oxyprenolol or a harmless placebo. On the ratings of two professional musician judges, the drug caused a significant improvement in performance. Not only that, but the drugged performers felt less jittery too.

It is a symptom of the slowness of society to recognize and utilize the beneficial results of academic research that international music competitions are still allowed to continue without dope tests.

If you do not want to drug your musicians into playing better, then you can lie to them about what music they are playing. Weick, Gilfillian and Keith (1973) did just that with two jazz bands. They were each asked to rehearse two new pieces, each piece accompanied by a press blurb about its arranger. One blurb was highly serious and complimentary, the other suggested an arranger of little merit or experience. In fact both pieces of music were by the same arranger, and they were of similar style, difficulty and musical value. The first band was given piece A with the good blurb, piece B with the bad blurb; the second band had the blurbs reversed.

"Perhaps if I sold the cello, I could afford a music stand."

For each band, the supposedly inferior piece of music was worse performed, badly remembered and less well-liked.

MUSICAL ABILITY

Van Alstyne and Osborne in a 1937 study ("Rhythmic responses of Negro and White children two to six") reported that black children were markedly superior to white children in clapping in time to a rhythmic apparatus. Sward in 1933 ("Jewish Musicality in America") found that Jewish children were slightly more musical than non-Jewish ones. Igaga in 1974 ("A comparative development study of the rhythmic sensitivity of Ugandan and English schoolchildren") found English children superior up to the age of 14, but Ugandans more musical thereafter. Ugandan girls scored better than boys on the measures of musical aptitude. Meanwhile, in Japan, Yamamatsu in 1974 showed that the rhythmic abilities of the Japanese had improved considerably between 1957 and 1967. Blacketer-Simmonds in 1953 tested the rhythmic abilities of 42 mongols and a similar number of mentally defective non-mongols. On being required to repeat simple patterns of drum-beats, 18 mongols and 14 non-mongols were reported to show "a good sense of rhythm." Cantor and Girardeau (1959) and Peters (1969) have done further tests on the musical abilities of defectives, but these studies produced no evidence that mongoloid children have any special musical capacities.

So to summarize: if we want musical aptitude with particular emphasis on rhythmic ability, we should be looking for a black, Jewish, Ugandan girl, over 14, living in Japan and probably not suffering from Down's syndrome.

Now firmly in ethnic territory, we move on to the next topic.

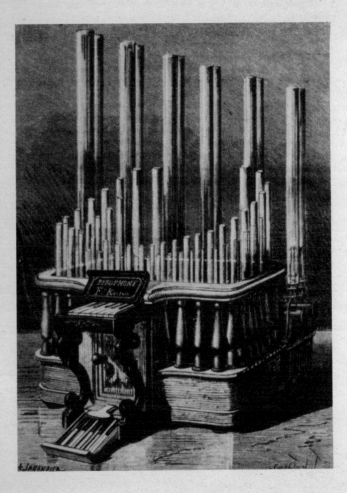

The Pyrophone—a hot-air organ.

ETHNOMUSICOLOGY

Dance ethnology is a relatively recent subject to come under the scrutiny of researchers, so we shall limit our observations to Tongan dance and the Apache Rabbit Dance.

In Tongan dance, according to Kaeppler (1972), *absence of exaggerated movement of the hips is considered significant*. The parts of the body which do have significant movements are the head, legs and arms. Though the head is important, its only significant movement is a quick tilt to the right. (The quick tilt back to the vertical may also be considered important, though Kaeppler does not mention it.) There are 11 important leg movements, but these are all movements of the lower leg. *"Although the upper leg certainly does move when taking steps or bending, it moves always as a result of movement of the lower leg and never for itself."* It is not considered in good taste in Tonga to expose or noticeably move the part of the body between waist and knee. Women who move this part of the leg are considered vulgar.

Arm movements are not so simple. All working parts appear to move. Quite apart from wrist and elbow swivels, there are 5 directions for the palm to face, 6 finger positions and 17 arm positions.

Regrettably, Kolinski (1972), in his otherwise thorough treatment of the Apache Rabbit Dance Song Cycle, as performed by the Iroquois, neglects the dance element in favor of a melodic and rhythmic analysis, complete with words. (Ha o o ha wi yo hè hè wi è hè i è yo ho wi yu ho hu—that's enough, they are meant to be nonsense syllables anyway). So we cannot draw any conclusions from a comparison of Tongan and Apache dance styles.

It is worth mentioning, however, that whereas only the

men of the Iroquois take part in the War Dance (to the same music as the Rain Dance), only the women perform the Old Time Shuffle Dance.

Finally, ethnomusicologically speaking, if you want a real challenge in a relatively unexplored field, then Pictish music can be thoroughly recommended. The problem of Pictish music, as explained by Porter (1983), is that there is no clear evidence that there was any. Practically nothing is known about the Picts anyway, except that they hung around the extremities of Scotland for several hundred years until their language died out in the ninth century A.D. All the musicologist has to go on are a few pictures of harps, lyres and pipes etched on stone. As James Porter explains, outlining the difficulties in his chosen field:

> Ethnomusicologists in any case have always held that their research should move beyond a circumscribed, post-Hellenic notion of ''music'' as a separate aesthetic concept . . . The framework for ''historical'' and ''synchronic'' ethnomusicology alike must be, as a consequence, interdisciplinary.

Of course, that makes it much simpler. But the interdisciplinary approach does enable a clear conclusion to be drawn: ''The Picts *may* have made an outstanding contribution to the history of Western music by developing the frame harp from Eastern or continental prototypes.'' (Not the author's italics.)

A topic more rich in research material than Pictish music was explored by Jansons (1986) in his thesis on ''The Problem of Classifying Latvian Folk Music.'' The Folklore Institute of Latvia contains 1,011,482 folk-song texts in its

Dodo doing Apache Rabbit Dance.

archives. There are also 28,488 melodies. The author notes sadly that *"Research in Latvian folk music has been carried out in an isolated atmosphere and published primarily in Latvian."* Fortunately, the study shows that the system de-

veloped by Béla Bartók for classifying Hungarian folk songs
can be modified to cope with Latvian ones too.

MUSICAL INSTRUMENTS

Everything you always wanted to know about E-flat tubas
may be found in Swain (1986) whose exhaustive catalog of
the 150 such instruments in the "Shrine to Music" museum
at the University of South Dakota is a model of its type. With
measurements of bore diameter, valve slide lengths, bell diameter, weight, height and other constructional details it must
be one of the few works devoted entirely to the tuba.

MOZART

Being a genius, Mozart has had many lesser mortals dis-
secting his life and work in order to reduce his talent to
manageable commodities. P. A. Malone (1981) has a fairly
typical thesis title: "Usage of trills and appoggiaturas in
W. A. Mozart's *Oboe Concerto in C* and *Oboe Quartet*."
Or, if you prefer a more intellectual approach, there is the
work of R. E. Atlas (1983): "The Diachronic Recognition
of Enharmonic Equivalence: A theory and its application to
five instrumental movements by W. A. Mozart" (in two vol-
umes).

But to end this chapter on a piece of true inconsequenti-
ality, I cannot resist quoting a formula devised by R. P. and
J. R. Cody and published in the *Journal of Irreproducible
Results* in 1986. It is the only piece of admittedly nonserious
research in this book, and is offered as an easy guide for
those who cannot remember the Köchel numbers of Mozart's
symphonies. The formula is:

The chamber flute-orum, a nineteenth-century instrument sadly neglected
by modern musicians.

$$S = .027465 + .157692K + .000159446K^2$$

It may be used to calculate any Mozart symphony number (S) from its Köchel number (K) and will give an answer not more than two out 85% of the time.

REFERENCES

Cantor, G. N. and Girardeau, F. L. (1959). "Rhythmic discrimination ability in mongoloid children." *American J. Mental Deficiency*, 63, 621–5.

Flugrath, J. M. (1969). "Modern-day rock-and-roll music and damage-risk criteria." *J. Acoustical Soc. America*, 45, 704–11.

Gregory, A. H. (1978). "Perception of clicks in music." *Perception and Psychophysics*, 24, 171–4.

Guettinger, H. R. (1985). "Consequences of domestication on the song structures in the canary." *Behaviour*, 94.

Haddon, E. (1952). "Possible origin of the Chopi Timbila xylophone." *African Music Soc. Newsletter*, 1, 61–7.

Hickerson, J. C. (1971). "Song folios and related resources in hillbilly music." *Western Folklore*, 30, 202–5.

Hood, M. (1966). "Slendro and Pelog redefined." *Selected Reports in Ethnomusicology*, UCLA, 1, 36–48.

James, I. M., Griffith, D. N. W., Pearson, R. M. and Newbury, P. (1977). "Effect of Oxyprenolol on stage-fright in musicians." *The Lancet*, 2, 952–4.

Jansons, A. (1986). "The problem of classifying Latvian folk music." Ed. D. thesis, State Univ. New Jersey.

Kaeppler, A. L. (1972). "Method and theory of analysing dance structure with an analysis of Tongan dance." *Ethnomusicology*, 16, 173–217.

Kolinski, M. (1972). "An Apache rabbit song dance cycle as sung by the Iroquois." *Ethnomusicology*, 16, 415–64.

Merriam, A. (1967). *Ethnomusicology of the Flathead Indians*. Chicago.

Mitani, J. C. (1985). "Gibbon song duets and intergroup spacing." *Behaviour*, 92.

Peters, M. (1969). "A comparison of the musical sensitivity of mongoloid and nonmongoloid children." Ph.D. thesis, Univ. of Illinois.

Porter, D. and Neuringer, A. (1984). "Music discrimination by pigeons." *J. Experimental Psychology*, 10.

Porter, J. (1983). "Harps, pipes and silent stones. The problem of Pictish music." *Selected Reports in Ethnomusicology*, 4, 243–67.

Rauhe, H. (1969). "Der Jazz als Objekt interdisziplinärer Forschung: Aufgaben und Probleme einer systematischen Jazzwissenschaft." *Jazzforschung*, 1, 23–61.

Shuter, R. (1974). "Singing out of tune: A review of recent research on this problem and its educational implications." *Scientific Aesthetics*, 9, 115–20.

Spector, J. (1966). "Classical *Ud* music in Egypt with special reference to Maqamat." *Ethnomusicology*, 14, 243–57.

Swain, J. J. (1986). "A catalog of the E-flat tubas in the Arne B. Larson collection at the University of South Dakota." Ph.D. thesis, Michigan State Univ.

Weick, K. E., Gilfillian, D. P. and Keith, T. A. (1973). "The effect of composer credibility on orchestra performance." *Sociometry*, 36, 435–62.

Zenatti, A. (1975). "Melodic memory tests: A comparison of normal children and mental defectives." *J. Research in Music Education*, 23, 41–52.

Standard tuning forks and musical spoons are preserved in the National
Physics Laboratory in Paris.

Chapter Eleven

Humor

The subject of humor is no laughing matter. A complete bibliography of all the papers and dissertations on humor* would comprise well over 2,000 items and range through psychology, sociology, anthropology, philosophy, literature, linguistics, semiotics and anything else which happens to be the trendy science of the day. We must first, however, define our terms.

Henri Bergson (in *Le Rire*, 1900) found the characteristic of humor to be "a certain mechanical inelasticity just where one would expect to find the wide-awake adaptability and the living pliableness of a human being."

Arthur Schopenhauer in 1818 had preferred the more abstract characterization of humor as "the incongruity between a concept and the real object which it was designed to relate." As an example he quoted the humorous riddle: "What is the angle between a circle and its tangent?" which apparently never failed to have old Schopenhauer falling about helpless with laughter. (Either this joke is not flattered by translation, or German humor really is as heavy as they say.)

In *fact, most of this research has been into the subject of humor rather than Humor*. There is a good deal of evidence to suggest that humor is less funny than Humor, but no serious research has yet been undertaken on the topic.

Having defined "Humor," we move on to the question of an individual's reaction to it. This we term "laughter."

"Laughter," wrote Immanuel Kant in 1790, "is an affectation arising from a sudden transformation of strained expectation into nothing."

"Laughter," wrote J. M. Rauleir in 1900, "consists of spasmodic contractions of the large and small zygomatic muscles and sudden relaxations of the diaphragm accompanied by contractions of the larynx and epiglottis."

Dr. F. R. Stearns in 1972 pointed out that laughing, if you do it properly, involved the cricothyroid and thyroartenoid muscles of the larynx, as well as the whole system of expiratory muscles: abdominal, lumbar, internal intercostal, subcostal, and transverse thoracic, together perhaps with a reverberation through some neuronic feedback network.

Apter and Smith (1978) tried to put humour and laughter together by identifying the conditions under which the former causes the latter. They identify three conditions necessary for a person to feel humour:

1. *He (or she) is in a paratelic state;*
2. *A synergy occurs involving two aspects of one situation;*
3. *It is sudden.*

(To understand all this, it is sufficient to know that "paratelic" means receptive to arousal; "synergy" is the mutually enhancing coincidence of two cognitive opposites. So the whole thing means that you experience humor if you're feeling giggly anyway and something funny happens.)

* * *

The centuries of effort put into finding an acceptable definition of the topic of humor have perhaps best been encapsulated by the contemporary philosopher and genius Mel Brooks, who explained succinctly: "Tragedy is if I cut my finger. Comedy is if you walk into an open sewer and die."

With that definition in mind, let us proceed to some of the recent findings. We divide the subject into Theoretical Humor and Applied Humor.

THEORETICAL HUMOR

Jane R. Littman (1983) presented a theory of humor and an explication of the concept of humor, in terms of an analysis of the relation of humor to emotional behavior. The parameters of successful *versus* unsuccessful humor were investigated and a status-dynamic analysis undertaken of the appreciation and enjoyment of humor. (Well, what she actually did was to get 35 undergraduates to rate 30 jokes.) Her conclusion was that the more seriously you take something, the more potential there is to enjoy humor about it. Provided, of course, you can see the funny side.

A specific example of this theme may be found in J. A. Thorson's 1985 paper ("A funny thing happened on the way to the morgue . . .") in the journal *Death Studies*.

Since most people do take death seriously, it ought to have high humor potential. Thorson's taxonomy of death jokes does indeed suggest a wide variety: Undertakers, Funerals, Burial, Necrophilia, Cannibalism, Death Scenes and Last Words, Memories of the Departed and Grief, Suicide and Homicide, Gallows Humor, and Death Personified.

He takes the line that death humor is a defense mechanism. This is all, however, surely too simple. A more serious

Necrophilia is a category of Death Humor.

approach to humor is found in T. L. Warburton's profound thesis of 1984: "Towards a Theory of Humor: An Analysis of the Verbal and Non-verbal Codes in Pogo."

Pogo, for the uninitiated, is an American comic strip featuring a possum called Pogo. In order to account for the mirth experience, the author introduced the notion of a comedic frame. The mirth experience is based on the audience's perception of the diction and action dimensions of the

Forbidden sex is a category in the Taxonomy of Humor.

comic strip. *The comedic frame exists when the diction dimension is perceived as acceptable and the specific manifestations of the action dimension are perceived as nonconsequential. When the comedic frame is recognized and accepted by the audience and anomaly exists within the comedic frame, humor results.*

So now you know. Additionally, Norman H. Holland quotes a valuable description of recent trends in research:

"Experiments now in progress hope to establish whether fewer than three dimensions of value normative anticonformity suffice to generate incongruity humor, and whether the minimum number of required dimensions anticonformed to depends upon if the norms violated represent ego-involving values or non-ego-involving beliefs."

. . . Specific manifestations of the action dimension are perceived as
nonconsequential . . .

Until this important question is answered, we shall not know whether to laugh.

APPLIED HUMOR

The study of laughter dates back at least to 1561 when the Abbé Domascere explained how different types of laughter corresponded to different personalities. A hi-hi-hi laugh indicated a melancholic personality, a ho-ho-ho was more sanguine, while a hee-hee-hee characterized a phlegmatic type, and a ha-ha-ha was positively choleric.

This rather subjective observation went unchallenged until 1980, when Miss P. A. Mitford undertook a doctoral thesis on "The Perception of Laughter and Its Acoustical Properties."

Fifteen female and 15 male subjects were persuaded to part with samples of laughter. From each subject, 4 different types of laughter were elicited: social laughter, tension-releasing laughter, humor-provoked laughter and tickling-induced laughter. The 120 laugh samples thus collected were analyzed in 2 different ways: objectively, using a real-time spectral analyzer; and subjectively, by being played to another group of 30 students who were asked to identify the sex of the laugher and the type of laugh.

The conclusions were not strong, but supported the theory that tension-release laughter is similar to social laughter, while humor and tickling are also hard to distinguish, whether by acoustics or perception. The listening group was also rather unsuccessful in judging the sex of the laughs presented to them.

Further research on the subject of tickling has shown that

a baby laughs more when tickled by its mother than when tickled by anyone else.

And a final important result concerning the infectious nature of social laughter: *Women on a diet are less influenced by the laughter of others in an audience than women not on a diet.*

Before leaving the subject of humor altogether, we should say a few words on the specialized topic of sexual humor, which has been defined, rather unnecessarily, as "any verbal joke which contains an explicit or implicit reference to sexual intercourse" (Raskin 1984).

Here the taxonomy breaks down the field into thematic subject areas: Genital Size, Prowess, Sexual Exposure, Sexual Ignorance, and Forbidden Sex. On the topic of Genital Size, Raskin points out that possible variations of size of organ, within certain limits, are part of every native speaker's internalized semantic script. *In sexual humor, this information, which is clearly part of the native speaker's linguistic competence, is supplemented, or rather superseded by a schematic binary mythological convention internalized as a specific sexual script:*

	(Normal = Neutral)
GENITAL SIZE (Male)	Gigantic = Good
	Small = Bad
	Gigantic = Bad
GENITAL SIZE (Female)	Normal = Neutral
	(Small = Good?)

(The lines in parentheses do not seem to be of any use in sexual humor.)

A gigantic organ.

We trust this helps explain things, though it may cast little light on the following poem, an example of the Russian chastushka. As the reader will notice, the verse form is a quatrain of typical trochaic four-footers, with the even lines lacking the last unstressed syllable.

Dyevki v ozere kupalis
Khuy rezinoviy nashli
Tsely dyen oni ebalis
Dazhe v shkolu nye poshli

As usual, the speaker is present, implicitly or explicitly, in the text and an analysis of the humor (which appears to improve with alcohol) sheds some light (or so it is claimed) on the dirty-joke taxonomy outlined above.

We might also care to compare this Russian poem-joke with an example (Vatuk 1968) of humor among the Hindi speaking children of North India:

a:da: pa:da: kisne pa:da:
ra:ja:ji:ka ghori ne pa:da:
thim tha:m thus

Even for the non-Hindi speaker, the onomatopoetic evocation of farting in the last line can hardly be missed. The whole verse translates as "Someone farted. Who farted? The King's horse farted!"

And in case your Russian is a bit rusty, a translation follows of that hilarious chastushka:

The girls were bathing in the lake
And found a rubber prick [dildo].
They fucked [themselves with it] for the whole day
So that they even missed school.

REFERENCES

Bradshaw, J. (1976). "Verbal jokes as de-transformed utterances and as speech acts." In: Chapman and Foot, 61–4.

Brukman, J. (1975). "Tongue Play: Constitutive and interpretive properties of sexual joking encounters among the Koya of South India." In: *Sociocultural Dimensions of Language*

. . . victimized protagonists and severity of misfortune . . .

Use. M. Sanches and B. Blount (Eds.). Academic Press, New York, 235–69.

Cantor, J. R. and Zillman, D. (1973). "Resentment towards victimized protagonists and severity of misfortune they suffer as factors in humor appreciation." *J. Exper. Res. in Personality*, 6, 321–9.

Chapman, A. J. and Foot, H. C. (1976). *Humour and Laughter: Theory, Research and Applications*. London.

Fine G. A. (1976). "Obscene joking across cultures." *Journ. of Communication*, 26, 134–40.

Giles, H. and Oxford, G. S. (1970). "Towards a multidimensional theory of laughter causation and its social implications." *Bull. Brit. Psychol. Soc.*, 22, 97–105.

Hall, G. S. and Allin, A. (1897). "The psychology of tickling, laughing and the comic." *Amer. J. Psychol.*, 9, 1–41.

Hoa, N. D. (1955). "Double puns in Vietnamese: A case of 'linguistic play.' " *Word*, 11, 237–44.

Holland, N. N. (1982). *Laughing. A Psychology of Humour.* Cornell Univ. Press.

Littman, J. R. (1983). "A new formulation of humour." *Advances in Descriptive Psychology*, 3, 183–207.

Milner, G. B. (1972). "Homo Ridens: Towards a semiotic theory of laughter." *Semiotica*, 5, 1–30.

Milford, P. A. (1980). "Perception of laughter and its acoustical properties." Doctoral thesis, Pennsylvania State Univ.

Murray, H. A., (1934). "The psychology of humour. 2. Mirth responses to disparagement jokes as a manifestation of an aggressive disposition." *J. Abnormal and Social Psychol.*, 29, 66–81.

Rapp, A. (1974). "Towards an eclectic and multilateral theory of laughter and humour." *J. General Psychol.*, 36, 207–19.

Rapp, A. (1949). "A pylogenetic theory of wit and humour." *J. Social Psychol.*, 30, 81–96.

Raskin, V. (1984). *Semantic Mechanisms of Humour*, D. Reidel Publ. Co., Holland.

Rothbart, M. K. and Pien, D. (1977). "Elephants and marshmallows: a theoretical synthesis of incongruity-resolution and arousal theories of humour." In: Chapman and Foot, 37–40.

Sperling, S. J. (1953). "On the psychodynamics of teasing." *J. Amer. Psychoanalytic Assoc.*, 1, 458–83.

Thorson, J. A. (1985). "A funny thing happened on the way to the morgue: some thoughts on humour and death, and a taxonomy of the humour associated with death." *Death Studies*, 9, 201–16.

Van Hooff, J. A. R. A. M. (1972). "A comparative approach to the phylogeny of laughter and smiling." In: *Non-Verbal Communication*, R. A. Hinde (Ed.), Cambridge, Eng.

Vatuk, V. P. (1968). "Let's dig up some dirt: The idea of humour in children's folklore in India." In: *Proc. 8th Int. Congress of Anthropol. and Ethnol. Sci.* vol 2, Tokyo.

Warburton, T. L. (1984). ''Toward a theory of humor: an analysis of the verbal and non-verbal codes in Pogo.'' Doctoral thesis, Univ. of Denver.

Chapter Twelve

Parapsychology

Perhaps a textbook of this nature ought not to include parapsychology. It is too obvious a target. Since the task of the parapsychologist is to investigate phenomena which cannot be explained by the traditional sciences, his work is by its very nature irrelevant to mainstream thought. Indeed his first task is to demonstrate the existence of events which science would rather did not exist at all.

In the good old days, parapsychology was an amalgam of clairvoyance, mysticism and spiritualism. It was all phantoms, psychics and premonitions. Even when the Society for Psychic Research was founded in 1882, they published mainly case studies of supposedly paranormal events, supporting the view that there was something beyond the confines of science, without actually going so far as to embrace religion.

Their methods, hovering uncomfortably between the anecdotal and empiric, could hardly be accused of claiming to possess scientific rigor. When Frederic Myers wrote his two-volume ''Human Personality and its Survival of Bodily Death'' (1903), he did not, in fact, interview any dead people to ask if their personalities had survived. K. Osis (1961) was also unable to gain access to the dead, but did the best he could by instigating a large-scale survey involving 640 doctors and nurses who were caring for terminal patients. In their last hours, 753 cases experienced an elevated mood,

(Mother Damnable)
(of KENTISH TOWN)
—— Anno 1676. ——
From a Unique Print in the Collection of L. Pinilly Esq.
Published by I. Caulfield 1793

Mother Damnable, a seventeenth-century parapsychologist.

888 reported "hallucinations of a non-human nature," and 1,370 saw apparitions, usually of deceased friends and relatives. The author interpreted the data as consistent with the hypothesis of life after death.

Of course, there is still room for doubt. Questionnaires given by doctors and nurses, probably untrained in proper scientific method, are hardly a reliable way to talk to the

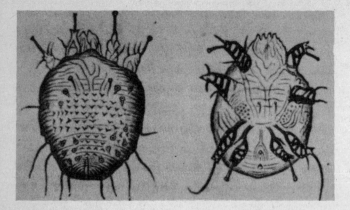

Parasitology, on the other hand, deals with fleas.

dead. The "elevated moods" reported could have been caused by post-questionnaire euphoria. And finally, the subjects weren't quite dead anyway.

These methodological objections could be overcome by a piece of work currently under way in the United States, where a group of researchers have designed an elaborate, coded system of messages to transmit to each other when they die. Unfortunately, at the moment (1987) all are in good health, so barring an altruistic gesture by one of the group, we may have to wait some time for the results.

Only slowly has parapsychology become established as an academic discipline. Perhaps the cloisters of academia have come to accept that this new subject can be investigated with proper scientific rigor. Or perhaps they have simply realized that it is no loonier than a lot of other things going on in the name of research. Whatever the reason, between 1930 and

1960 proper experimental techniques evolved for parapsychology. With superstition replaced by methodology, it became a worthy candidate for irrelevant research.

The two most important areas in this parascience are known as Extrasensory Perception (ESP) and Psychokinesis (PK) and are defined as follows:

ESP—Knowledge of or response to an external event or influence not apprehended through known sensory channels.

PK—The influence of mind on external objects or processes without the mediation of known physical energies or forces.

(So ESP is telepathy and precognition; PK includes mind-over-matter phenomena.)

Before lurching into the research in these two topics, we should mention one other important area, of great relevance to the interface between parapsychology and religion. We refer, of course, to *the effect of holy water on the growth of radish plants.*

A project at the University of Santa Clara, USA, in 1979 was devoted to establishing whether radishes nourished on holy water grew better than those watered from the tap. 24 radishes in peat pots were divided into 2 equal groups. 12 were then watered with holy water, the other 12 with tap water. The mean growth rate of each group was calculated. No significant differences were discovered.

The lady responsible for this research points out two drawbacks: firstly, the man who watered them knew which group was which, so may have been subconsciously motivated to influence the result of the experiment; and secondly, the holy water suffered from being stored in aluminium containers and was only changed weekly. "Future studies would be improved were such factors controlled." We look forward eagerly to further results, but might suggest that some measurements ought also to be taken of the moral health of the radishes—and indeed of those who eat them.

Putting radishes behind us, let us proceed to the land of ESP.

Rémy Chauvin was the first to do serious research into ESP in mice. He published his results under a pseudonym (Pierre Duval) perhaps to keep the mice guessing. His experimental device was a cage, divided into two halves, either of which could be electrified. The impending electric shock would always be signalled by a central light, inviting the mice in the cage to guess which side of the cage to opt for. Which side actually received the shock was, in fact, determined at random.

So the mice ought to receive a shock 50% of the time. In fact it was found that their shock rate was significantly lower. Chauvin's explanation was they had some "precognition" of the event, that the mice "knew" which side of the cage was about to be electrified.

This was an historic experiment, giving rise to numerous developments. The first question was whether the result was a true demonstration of ESP. According to one noted parapsychologist, *there was another conceivable explanation: that of paranormal action by the mouse on the electronic apparatus itself*. The mouse was not, in fact, guessing which side the shock would come, it was influencing the random event generator which allocated the shocks. It was not ESP but PK.

A similar confusion reigns concerning a classic experiment by R. L. Morris in 1967. He put three goldfish in a tank, monitored their movements, and occasionally fished one out with a net. Which of the goldfish was to be picked up was determined by a dice throw by another experimenter. His results showed that a goldfish about to be netted was significantly more active than its unmolested colleagues.

Were the goldfish showing precognition of the dice throws? Or were the experimenters psychokinetically influencing the dice? Or perhaps the goldfish were psychokinetically influencing the dice. Five years later, Morris did a similar experiment using random number tables instead of dice to determine which goldfish were to be caught in the net. The results on that occasion were not significant, suggesting that goldfish may not have telepathic powers after all.

A brief divergence might be appropriate here into the effects of psychokinesis on dice. Much research has been done to demonstrate that PK can be used to influence dice throws, but the mechanism of this influence is not properly understood. An intriguing experiment (Carroll, 1981) involved 4 experimenters, each with 24 subjects. Each subject released 3 pairs of dice 144 times, attempting to influence one pair to read high and another pair to read low. The third pair functioned only as a control. Overall scores supported the view that such influences were indeed acting: the high-aim dice scored higher than the controls, which in turn scored higher than the low-aim. The results were analyzed to test for simultaneous success on both high-aim and low-aim dice, but this did not happen with greater frequency than such successes on single rolls. The conclusion was that the results did not indicate that PK acted on more than one die per roll.

This apparent deficiency in the powers of the psychokineticist may sound rather enfeebling, but we should also consider the result of Averill and Rhine (1945) on the effect of alcohol upon performance in PK tests. Each of three subjects rolled 96 dice at a time for 20 trials "attempting to will or volitionally influence the dice to come up sixes." By chance one would expect a rate of 4 sixes per 24 throws; in fact their success score was an average of 4.39 sixes per 24 throws.

Then, 2 of the subjects each ingested* 100 cc of gin and attempted to repeat the experiment. Their average score for sixes dropped to 4.06. The conclusion was that alcohol impairs PK efficiency. But the 1981 result might shed new light on this interpretation. If the PK can only operate on one die at a time, then it might be considered quite a success for it to reach its mark at all under conditions of blurring vision and alcoholic haze. After all, 4.09 is still above average.

To return to the question of ESP, or possibly PK, effects among animals. The literature is too vast to give full coverage, but we should mention that Schmidt in 1970 found that a heat lamp controlled by a random number generator stayed on longer when his pet cat had access to the area under the lamp. On the other hand he found that cockroaches on an electric grid were shocked more often than they ought to have been by the random number generator which controlled the grid. Watkins's (1971) results for lizards under a heat lamp appeared to depend on barometric pressure and humidity.

As in many other sciences, a good many rats have died in the cause of parapsychology. Morris (of goldfish netting fame) found evidence that rats were less likely to run around an open field if they were going to be killed in 10 minutes'

*Subjects, it should be noted, always ingest. Only common people drink.

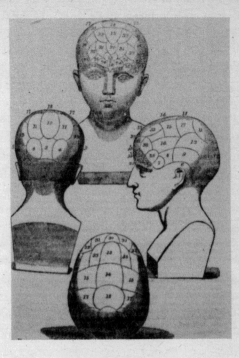

The art of phrenology.

time. (Random numbers, as usual, determined which rats were going to die.) This result may have been affected by the fact that all the rats had previously been used in another researcher's experiments and, but for Morris, would have been killed off even sooner.

Craig and Treurniet (1974) used a T-shaped maze to see if rats could correctly guess which way to turn at the top of the junction. As an incentive to guess right, a punishment of death was inflicted on the rats who went the wrong way.

Results were not significant, but it was observed that correct choices were usually preceded by longer thought. Treurniet and Craig (1975) later discovered a relationship between rats' making correct choices and the phase of the moon.

Killing rats might be considered rather an extreme punishment for a poor guess, but it has not proved easy to find good ways of motivating animals in such research. Depriving kittens of food has been found to improve their ESP scores, though only marginally, while giving them electric shocks en route to the food bowls has been claimed to kill off any ESP effects that might otherwise have existed. Much work has been done by Broughton and Millar (1975) on the topic of optimal conditioning of gerbils. Sunflower seeds are a good start.

Gruber (1979) obtained marginally significant results without using sunflower seeds, in an experiment to determine whether human willpower can influence the activity level of gerbils on a treadmill or in a box.

On another human–animal experiment, Helmut Schmidt, one of the leaders in this field, rewarded a dog with chocolates whenever a human subject made a correct guess in an ESP test. The dog (a 7-year-old miniature dachshund, supposedly nonpsychic) was thus motivated to influence the man's performance. Under these conditions, the man did indeed improve his scores. But the dog alone did best of all. Further experiments are planned.

In related experiments, Schmidt unfortunately failed to obtain measureable effects to demonstrate PK powers of algae, yeast cultures or fruit flies.

Finally, we come to plants. Backster (1968) has hypothesized a form of biological communication called ''primary

A dog influencing the throw of dice.

perception'' possessed by all living cells. *To test this hypothesis, he monitored the electrical resistance on philodendron leaves to see if they responded to the death of a distant brine shrimp.* Shrimps were dumped into boiling water at times decided, as usual, by a random event generator. The plant responses were monitored, the whole procedure being automated and everything going on in the absence of experi-

"I'll ask you once more: Did you sense the death of a nearby shrimp?"

menters with only the philodendra and the shrimps knowing the awful truth.

The results, according to Backster, showed significantly more activity from the plant during time periods when shrimps were dying. Later researchers, however, have failed to replicate this finding.

As with so many areas in this important subject, more research is clearly needed.

REFERENCES

Averill, R. L. and Rhine, J. B. (1945). "The effect of alcohol upon performance in PK tests." *J. Parapsychology*, 9, 32–41.

Backster, C. (1968). "Evidence of a primary perception in plant life." *Internat. J. Parapsychology*, 10, 329–48.

Bestall, C. M. (1962). "An experiment in precognition in the laboratory mouse." *J. Parapsychology*, 26, 269.

Braud, W. G. and Kirk, J. (1978). "Attempt to observe psychokinetic influence upon a random event generator by person–fish teams." *European J. Parapsychology*, 2, 228–36.

Broughton, R. and Millar, B. (1975). "An attempted confirmation of the rodent ESP findings with positive reinforcement." *European J. Parapsychology*, 1, 15–35.

Craig, J. G. and Treurniet, W. (1974). "Precognition in rats as a function of shock and death." *Research in Parapsychology*, 1973, 75–78.

Duval, P. and Montredon, E. (1968). "ESP experiments with mice." *J. Parapsychology*, 32, 153–66.

Flew, A. (1956). "Can a man witness his own funeral?" *Hibbert Journal*, 54, 242–52.

Gale, R. M. (1965). "Why a cause cannot be later than its effect." *Review of Metaphysics*, 19, 209–34.

Gruber, E. R. (1979). "Conformance behaviour involving animal and human subjects." *European J. Parapsychology*, 3, 36–50.

Horowitz, K. A., Lewis, D. C. and Gasteiger, E. L. (1975). "Plant 'primary perception': electro-physiological unresponsiveness to brine shrimp killing." *Science*, 189, 478–80.

Lenington, S. (1979). "The effect of holy water on the growth of radish plants." *Psychological Reports*, 45, 381–2.

Metta, L. (1972). "Psychokinesis in lepidopterus larvae." *J. Parapsychology, 36, 213–21*.

Nash, C. B. (1981). "Simultaneous high and low aim in the same roll of dice." *J. Amer. Soc. Psychical Res.*, 75, 259–66.

Osis, K. (1961). *Deathbed observations by physicians and nurses.* Parapsychology Foundation, New York.

Osis, K. and Foster, E. B. (1953). "A test of ESP in cats." *J. Parapsychology*, 17, 168–86.

Parker, A. (1974). "ESP in gerbils using positive reinforcement." *J. Parapsychology*, 38, 308–11.

Schmidt, H. (1983). "Superposition of PK Effects by Man and Dog." *Research in Parapsychology*.

Treurniet, W. C. and Craig, J. G. (1975). "Precognition as a function of environmental enrichment and time of the lunar month." *Research in Parapsychology*, 1974, 100–102.

Watkins, G. K. (1971). "Possible PK in the lizard *Anolis sagrei*." *Proc. Parapsychological Assoc*.

Section Two

Knowledge at a Glance

The topics already discussed in this book have reflected the growth of man's thirst for knowledge. As we have seen, Alcohol has played its small part in assuaging that thirst. But the lust for scientific discovery has continued unabated, a lust which even Courtship and Sex have been unable to satisfy completely.

The major subject areas which we have tackled up to this point can give us a good grasp of mainline research, but still leave a vast amount of ground uncovered. This section is therefore a sprint through the rest of the material—a quick trim round the fringes of learning. Arranged alphabetically, and fully cross-referenced, it also serves as an index to the earlier material in this book.

A

ABDOMINAL HAIRS

For a discussion of the role of abdominal hairs in the material behavior of wolf spiders, the reader is referred to the paper by J. S. Rovner, G. A. Higashi and R. F. Foelix: "Material behaviour in wolf spiders: the role of abdominal hairs," *Science*, 1973, 182, 98–119.

The role of facial hairs in maternal behavior has yet to be explained.

ADOLESCENCE

The potentially valuable role of video games in an adolescent's development is discussed under *Video Games*.

The occurrence of explicitly drawn breasts in adolescent girls' pictures of human figures is discussed in **BODIES**. (p. 106).

AGGRESSION

The effects of aggression on sexual behavior of crows and grouse is discussed in **SEX** (pp. 84–5).

The role of pheromones in inhibiting aggression in spiders is discussed in **SPIDERS** (p. 60).

For aggression in the Crayfish, see *Crayfish*.

ALCOHOL

A full treatment of this subject will be found in **ALCOHOL**. For further information the reader is referred to: **CHICK-**

ENS (p. 47), for the effect of alcohol on the maternal instincts of cocks; **SPIDERS** (p. 60) for the effect of washing spiders or crickets in alcohol on the behavior of other spiders; **PARAPSYCHOLOGY** (p. 152) for the effect of alcohol on the ability to throw dice successfully.

ALGAE
A group of Thallophytes including seaweeds and other forms. Whether they can be influenced by telepathic methods appears doubtful. See **PARAPSYCHOLOGY** (p. 154).

ANGULAR MOMENTUM
For an interesting question concerning a possibly serious violation of the Law of Conservation of Angular Momentum, see *Diving*.

ANT
A good description of the leg movements of ants while swimming is to be found in a 1985 paper by M. B. DuBois and R. Jander (*Physiol. Entomol.*, vol. 10, no. 3) entitled: Leg Coordination and Swimming in an Ant, *Camponotus Americanus*. The authors conclude that swimming in ants is an activity which can be derived from walking. The major difference in leg movements is a suppression of the rhythmic movements of the middle and hind legs.

APACHE RABBIT DANCE
A dance which has been observed performed by the Iroquois. See **MUSIC** (p. 125).

An Ant.

ARISTOTLE
Greek philosopher (384–322 B.C.) with strange views about women and teeth. See **SEX** (p. 76).

ARM
A part of the body which does not feature among the top half-dozen in its contribution to self-esteem (see **BODIES** p. 108). Its contribution to speed in the front crawl swimming stroke, however, (see *Swimming*) suggests the need for further research to see whether freestyle swimmers esteem their arms more greatly than breast-strokers.

ASPHYXIATION
Deprivation of air, which may be done postnatally to dogs (see **SYNCHRONIZED DROWNING**) or prenatally to guinea pigs (see *Guinea pig*).

ASTHMA
An account of asthma attacks brought on by the sight of fish is to be found in **GOLDFISH** (p. 26).

B

BABOON
The question of whether female chacma baboons have orgasms is discussed under *Orgasm*.

BACH
Johann Sebastian (1685–1750). Composer of organ pieces and works of the flute which have had a profound influence on the musical appreciation of pigeons. See **MUSIC** (pp. 118–9).

BACTERIA
See *Underclothes*.

BANANA PLANT
For an interesting explanation of how a male spider finds a female spider in a banana plant while loud noises are being played at them by psychologists, see **SPIDERS** (pp. 62–4).

BATS
A great deal of work has been done on how bats' radar works to identify and catch other insects for food. D. R. Griffin, F. A. Webster and C. R. Michael gave the answers in 1960 (*Animal Behaviour*, 8, 141–54) in their paper "The Echolocation of Flying Insects by Bats."

The skeleton of a bat.

In general, the whole procedure of detection, location and interception takes no more than half a second. Bats are especially good at catching mosquitoes and fruit flies, sometimes averaging 10 mosquitoes or 14 fruit flies every minute. (When they are catching them at this rate, the method used to estimate numbers is to weigh the bat before and after eating.)

During the search phase, the frequency of the bat's shriek starts at 100 kilocycles and drops to 50 in each pulse of sound. The pulses are emitted at intervals of 50–100 milliseconds.

During the approach phase, there is a progressive shortening of intervals, though the frequencies remain the same. In the terminal phase the pulse duration drops to half a millisecond at intervals of 5 or 6 milliseconds. The frequency also drops, sometimes to as low as 25–30 kilocycles.

A bat can detect Drosophila up to 50 cm away, but a fruit fly or mosquito can be detected up to a meter away.

To see how moths manage to evade bats, see *Moths*.

BATHING
Something shelducks are liable to do if you interrupt them while they are copulating. See **SEX** (p. 81).

BEES
Bees are intelligent little buzzers (according to J. Gould and C. Gould in *New Scientist*, April 1983, 84). If you

move their food each day further away from the hive, in equal measured jumps, some of them begin to recognize the pattern and anticipate the next day's movement, hovering over the designated spot.

Crows have been found to be capable of the same reasoning.

According to A. Sengun ("Experimente zur Sexuell-mechanischen Isolation." *Rev. Fac. Sci.* Istanbul, 1944, 9, 239–53), there is some experimental evidence that surgical alteration of the male genitalia in bees may not impair or prevent their abilities to copulate or fertilize.

We await with interest the results of similar experiments on crows.

BEER BOTTLE
Sexual surrogate for Australian beetles. See **COURTSHIP** (pp. 91–2).

BEETLE
Sexual companion for Australian beer bottles. See **COURTSHIP** (pp. 91–2).

BERGSON
Henri Louis (1859–1941). French philosopher and Nobel

prizewinner in 1927. See **HU-MOR** (p. 133).

BERSERK

Old Norse warriors in the times of the sagas, taking their name from the original Berserk, who refused to don armor for battle, preferring to wear the bear skin or *ber-serk*. Recent research suggests that the frenzied power of the Berserks may be due to hallucinogenic drugs. See *Mushroom*.

Optic occlusion seen here not to preclude a leg-over situation.

BLINDFOLD

For the effect of a blindfold on the ability of a chick to recognize its mother hen, and its effect on the chick's fear of worms, see **CHICKENS** (p. 39).

BLINDING

A useful experimental device for determining the function of the eye. For the effect of blindness on the swimming speed of goldfish, see **GOLDFISH** (p. 23). For the effect of blindness on the problem-solving abilities of rats brought up in a restricted environment, see *Environment*. For the effect of blinding (by painting its eyes with black lacquer) on a spider's web-building, see **SPIDERS** (p. 65).

BLUEBIRD

For a rather odd mating experience with a bluebird, see **COURTSHIP** (p. 91).

BODIES

These are discussed extensively in **BODIES**, but see also *Arm, Leg, Eye, Penis,* etc.

BONDAGE

For the reaction of male butterflies to female virgins in

Studies in elephant literacy have made little progress.

bondage, see **COURTSHIP** (pp. 92–3).

For the reaction of hens to being swathed in bandages, see **CHICKENS** (p. 40).

BOOKS
Research has suggested that book publishers may be influenced by the potential sales of a book when deciding on its title. See *Literature*.

BRAIN
A general theory of the functioning of the brain will be found in **WORMS** (p. 51).

The effects on its memory of cutting out a goldfish's brain

will be found in **ALCOHOL** (p. 12).

A general discussion of the potential learning abilities of the goldfish brain will be found in **GOLDFISH** (pp. 21–2).

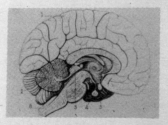

A brain.

For the effects of cutting out a chick's brain on its response towards the mother hen, see **CHICKENS** (p. 40).

The effects of injecting an uneducated rat's brain with extracts from an educated rat's brain are referred to in **WORMS** (p. 56).

For work connected with the octopus brain, see **GOLD-FISH** (pp. 24–5).

BREASTS

A great deal of information about human breasts, and the relationship of their owners and others to them, will be found in **BODIES**.

A useful study of rat breasts was done in 1966 by L. L. Roth and J. S. Rosenblatt whose results were published (*Science*, 151, 1403–4) under the title: "Mammary glands of pregnant rats: Development stimulated by licking."

Two groups of pregnant rats took part in the experiment. In the first group, the rats were unrestrained: in the second group, neck collars were attached to the rats in order to prevent them from licking their ventral surfaces. After the gestation period was over, the results showed that the mammary glands of the collar-wearers were on average 50%

less well developed than those of the animals allowed to lick.

BREEDING

Much relevant to this subject will be found in **SEX** and **COURTSHIP**. For some other breeding statistics, see *Hedgehog*.

BROOKS

Mel, born (Melvin Kaminsky) 1926. American philosopher and researcher into experimental media communications studies. See **HUMOR** (p. 135). A further useful reference is: Atlas, J. (1975), "Mel Brooks: The film director as fruitcake." *Film Comment*, 11, 54–7.

The Portrait of Mr MARTIN VAN BUTCHELL

BURIAL
See **HUMOR** (p. 135).

BUTCHELL
Martin van (1735–1812). Son
of Martin van Butchell, tap-
estry maker to George II. See
Taxidermy.

BUTTERFLY
A discussion of bondage fe-
tishism and butterfly foreplay
will be found in **COURT-
SHIP** (pp. 92–3).

A further cause of poten-
tially deviant behavior in butterflies will be found in:
Anderson, A. L. (1932). "The
sensitivity of the legs of common butterflies to sugars,"
*Journal of Experimental Zo-
ology*, 63, 235–9.

C

CANARY
The canary as songsmith is discussed in **MUSIC** (p. 119).

CANNABIS
If its effects on mice are anything to go by, the practice of taking cannabis cannot be recommended. See **SEX** (p. 85).

CANNIBALISM
For the effect of cannibalistic behavior on worm memory, see **WORMS** (pp. 55–6).

Cannibalism as a bad habit of the spider will be found in **SPIDERS** (pp. 59–60).

Cannibalism as a humor category is referred to in **HUMOR** (p. 135).

CASTRATION
The effects of castration on the sexual habits of mice, cats, dogs, guinea pigs, rats, hamsters and starlings will all be found in **SEX** (pp. 78–81).

The effect of genital surgery on bees may be found under *Bees*.

CATS
Whether anaesthetized cats feel pain when their testicles are squeezed is discussed under *Testicle*.

The ability of falling cats to land on their feet is mentioned under *Diving*.

The warmth-seeking behavior of cats who live with parapsychologists is discussed in **PARAPSYCHOLOGY** (p. 152).

How long it takes to drown a cat may be discovered in **SYNCHRONIZED DROWNING** (p. 30).

The sexual behavior of castrated cats is mentioned in **SEX** (p. 80).

CATATONIA
An extreme form of schizophrenia characterized by periods of stupor. The effect of feeding the blood of catatonics

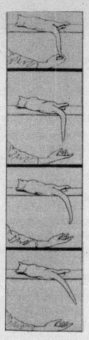

The mechanics of pulling a cat's tail.

to spiders will be found in **SPIDERS** (pp. 66–8).

CHAFFINCH
The effects on behavior and gender discrimination in chaffinches of dyeing a female's underpants* red will be found in **SEX** (pp. 77–8).

*A misprint for "underparts," too charming to correct.

CHEETAH
Cultural tastes of the cheetah are discussed in **MUSIC** (p. 118).

CHICKENS
Much of the state of current research into chickens will be found in **CHICKENS**. For a further reference to the intelligence of chickens, see *Intelligence*.

CHIMPANZEE
The important question of whether alcoholic chimpanzees suffer from hangovers can be found in **ALCOHOL** (p. 11).

CINEMA COMEDY
An important recent contribution to our knowledge of what makes a good funny film is Sikov, E. K. (1986 Doctoral dissertation, Columbia University): "Laughing Hysterically: American Screen Comedies of the 1950s."

The author analyzes films directed by Hawks, Wilder, Hitchcock and Tashlin, relating their content to the stylistic and thematic concerns of Hollywood films of the period. The films are viewed as paradigms of the popular cinema's potential for cogent and lucid criticism through art. The conclusion is that American screen comedy thrived during this period because the untenable repression which characterized America at the time demanded its own subversion.

I suppose that is why Mel Brooks's (q.v.) films are so funny too.

CIRCUMCISION
See **SEX** (p. 75).

CLOTHING
Have you ever wondered why people tend, in general, to wear matching tops and bottoms in suits? Or why men (except by accident) usually put on jackets and trousers from the same suit when dressing?

These phenomena were discussed in: "Meaning of Garments: The Relation between the Impression of an Outfit and the Message Carried by its Component Garments," by Gibbins, Keith and Schneider, (1980) *Perceptual and Motor Skills*, 51, 287–91.

The researchers investigated the hypothesis that the impression created by an outfit is the simple sum of its component garments. The 16 possible combinations of 4 tops and 4 bottoms were each rated by 54 judges aged between 18 and 51. Also the 8 individual component parts were rated. The outfits were not only rated for overall impression, but judged on each item of a 49-adjective scale, containing descriptions such as "adventurous," "reserved," "dull," etc.

In most cases, a relationship was found between the overall impression of the outfit and that of its component parts, but a linear model is inadequate to describe it. In other words, it has been demonstrated that an attractive jacket and attractive trousers do not necessarily add up to a nice suit.

COCA-COLA
A comparison of the contraceptive qualities of Original Coke, New Coke, Diet Coke and Caffeine-free Coke will be found in **COURTSHIP** (pp. 98–100).

COCKROACH
Whether cockroaches can avoid, by paranormal means,

randomly generated electric shocks, is a question which has never been fully resolved. When H. Schmidt (see **PARAPSYCHOLOGY** (p. 152) performed the experiment, he found that his experimental cockroaches in fact suffered more shocks than would have been expected. It has been suggested that Schmidt himself was paranormally influencing the electric shock generator, because he dislikes cockroaches. Equally, there could be a high degree of masochistic tendencies in the cockroach.

See *Earthquake* for further useful abilities of the cockroach.

COITUS INTERRUPTUS

The effects of coitus interruptus on ducks can be found in **SEX** (pp. 81–2), where information on interrupting rat coitus is also available.

COLOR

The effects of offering chickens the choice of food on blue circles, red triangles, blue triangles and red circles may be found in **CHICKENS** (p. 44).

A valuable experiment on the mechanism of color vision in the goldfish is outlined in **GOLDFISH** (p. 23).

Generally the favorite color of experimental psychologists seems to be red, as may be seen in **SEX**, where they dyed the underparts of female chaffinches red, and under *Robin*, where the effect of redlessness on a robin's breast was examined. In the same place the effect of red on sticklebacks and sticklefronts may be discovered.

What color orangutans like their food to be will be found under *Orangutan*. (One young orangutan, like psychologists, showed a fondness for red.)

Finally, the best colors for squash balls will be found under *Squash*.

CONTRACEPTION

The use of soft drinks as prophylactics will be found in **COURTSHIP** (pp. 98–100).

CONVERSATION

A current research topic in England, (for which a grant of £16,710 was awarded in 1986) investigates ''How Closing a Topic in Conversation is Socially Managed.'' Preliminary investigations established that when a topic of conversation is exhausted, there may be two relevant options for the ensuing course of the interaction: a definite move may be made to close the whole conversation, or a new topic may be begun by actively searching for something to keep the conversation going. (In other words: when you've run out of things to say about something, you either shut up or talk about something else.) The research in progress announces its aim as finding out why specifically closing a topic produces these two options.

Interruption of conversations, and why men do it more often than women, is discussed under *Sexism*. An unsuccessful attempt to interrupt spiders' conversations may be found in **SPIDERS** (pp. 62–4).

COPULATION
There is a lot of this going on in **SEX** and **COURTSHIP**, and some more in **CHICKENS** (pp. 44–5) and **SPIDERS** (pp. 61–2).

COURTSHIP
Discussed at length in **COURTSHIP**, further specialized references will be found in **CHICKENS** (p. 44), **SPIDERS** (pp. 61–2) and **BODIES** (p. 107).

CRAB
A brief remark pertinent to crabs will be found under *Intelligence*.

CRAYFISH
"The importance of aggression as a factor affecting temperature selection by crayfish has not been studied," announced S. K. Peck, who took it upon himself to rectify this serious omission. His results are reported in his 1985 paper: "Effects of aggressive interaction on temperature selection by the crayfish," (*Am. Midl. Nat.*, vol. 114 no. 1).

By placing crayfish, singly or in pairs, in an experimental tank in which the temperature of the water varied, he was able to ascertain how hot they like the water to be. When crayfish were placed together in the water, increased movements were reported, as well as more variability in their choice of temperature, compared with when they were alone.

CRICKET
For the reaction of spiders to crickets washed in alcohol and ether, see **SPIDERS** (p. 60).

CROW
For the inhibiting effect of aggression on the sexual habits of crows, see **SEX** (p. 84).

Various results on the intelligence of crows will be found under *Bees* and *Intelligence*.

CUCKOLDRY
For a sordid tale of urban cuckoldry in pied and collared flycatchers and useful tips on how to determine the paternity of illegitimate offspring, see **COURTSHIP** (pp. 94–5).

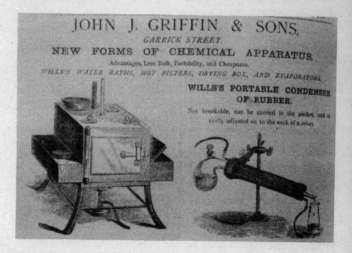

D

DANCING
Some advice concerning the merits of learning to dance for a young male spider will be found in **SPIDERS** (p. 61).

What to do, and not to do, with your hips, legs, arms, hands and fingers in Tongan dance will be found outlined in **MUSIC** (p. 125), where also are some lyrics for the Apache Rabbit Dance.

DEAFNESS
The effect of wearing earplugs on a chick's ability to recognize its mother hen may be found in **CHICKENS** (p. 39).

The effects of loud noise on the mating habits of deaf rats are discussed in **SEX** (p. 82).

DEATH
Moscow News Information, no. 95, 1983, reported interesting findings on the effect of death on mice. In laboratory tests, a white mouse was given a fatal drug in front of a dozen other mice. At the same time a mouse from a second group was also given a fatal drug dose, but not in front of other mice. This procedure was repeated several times. So one group of mice saw several of its number die, the other group merely saw them taken away, never to return.

The number of pregnant females subsequently recorded in the first group was nearly twice as large as that of the second group. The scientists concluded that certain connections exist between the perception of sudden and abnormal deaths within a group and the birth rate of the group.

That rats may also be adversely affected by death may be found in **PARAPSYCHOLOGY** (pp. 152–4). The same chapter contains a discussion of the long-term effects of death.

A taxonomy of the humorous side of death may be found in **HUMOR** (p. 135).

For a time and motion study of death by drowning, the reader is referred to **SYNCHRONIZED DROWNING**.

Further aspects of sudden death, in man and rat, may be found under *Voodoo*.

DECEPTION

How to be convincing when lying about your age in a bar is explained under *Eye contact*.

Useful tips on deception for chickens bent on seduction can be found in **CHICKENS** (pp. 46–7).

DEVIATION

A discussion of deviation and perversion in poultry may be found in **CHICKENS** (pp. 42–3).

Deviant behavior in butterflies is mentioned in **COURTSHIP** (p. 93).

Sexual deviations may be found in **SEX**, at various places, while the influence of alcohol on such deviations may be found in **ALCOHOL** (pp. 16–7).

Whether personal deviations are expressed in a sub-

ject's drawings is discussed in **BODIES** (p. 103).

DIETING

Experimental evidence to show that women on a diet are crabbier than women not on a diet may be found in **HUMOR** (p. 140).

See also *Cannibalism, Food,* etc.

DISCO MUSIC

The effect of loud disco music on the sexual orientation of mice and on the hearing abilities of pigs may be found in **SEX** (p. 85).

DISGUISE

The art of disguise is discussed in **CHICKENS** (p. 40).

DIVING

The question of whether divers violate the laws of physics was raised by C. Frohlich in his 1979 paper: "Do springboard divers violate angular momentum conservation?" (*Amer. J. Physics*, 47, 583–92).

The answer must be related to the analogous question: "How does a cat fall on its feet?," which was the title of a *New Scientist* article (1960, 1647-9) by D. McDonald.

The reader is referred to the closely related topic of the posture of a falling mouse, to be found under *Mouse*.

DOGS

In his excellent 1955 review of work on the effects of environmental restriction on the development of animals, D. O. Hebb ("The mammal and his environment," *Amer. J. Psychology*, 11, 826) attributes some interesting effects to the basic stupidity of dogs.

A test of canine intelligence.

To understand the results, we must start (as so often) with rats.

B. Hymovitch reared two groups of rats in different ways. Rats of the first group lived in small one-rat cages, with as much food and water as they wanted, but no exercise wheel, no socializing, no problems to solve and no pain. The second group lived in a free environment, with other rats and constant challenges and obstacles to overcome. The rats in the first group were shown to have a permanent inferiority in the ability to solve problems.

W. R. Thompson performed a similar experiment with dogs. Despite initial misgivings about depriving a Scottish terrier of stimulation, he proceeded with the experiment because the dog seemed to be thriving on it. In fact, the dogs which he brought up in a problem-free and isolated environment ate better, grew better and on release behaved more friskily than other dogs normally reared. The experimental dogs even won first prizes in local dog shows.

Hebb's conclusion is that the dogs behaved in that manner because after the early deprivation, they were excited at everything. They even paid no

A design for an experiment to show that a dog's gastric juices still flow if food is prevented from reaching the stomach.

attention to pain. Hyperactive and never bored, afraid of nothing, deprived dogs retain the charms of the frisky puppy. In fact, they had no fear and showed no pain simply because they were not smart enough. Dumb dogs make better pets.

The next question regarding deprivation of stimulation is what happens if we reverse the procedure? How does an animal brought up normally react to being deprived of stimulation later in life? An experiment on these lines was reported by W. H. Bexton, W. Heron and T. H. Scott in 1954 (*Canadian J. Psychology*, 8, 70). As D. O. Hebb explains: "This experiment is too cruel to do with animals, but not with college students."

Accordingly, students were paid to do nothing for 24 hours a day. The only excitement in their lives was eating and going to the toilet. They wore frosted glasses, letting in light but no pattern vision; they had sponge pillows over their ears; gloves with long cardboard cuffs covered their fingers to allow only minimal tactile stimulation. Their only communication was through loudspeakers embedded in their earmuffs.

In this sensory deprivation

state, they reported difficulty in concentrating, and showed an inability to solve simple problems. They found themselves looking forward to being given problems, for something to do, but when the problem arrived lethargy and quick loss of interest overcame them. Visual and auditory hallucinations were further symptoms reported.

Several of these effects persisted, including the poor problem-solving abilities, for some time after the subjects had emerged from the experimental cubicles.

Further research on the problem-solving abilities of dogs will be found under **Information Technology**.

Cruelty to dogs is explored in depth in **SYNCHRONIZED DROWNING**.

The effects of rewarding a nonpsychic dachshund with chocolates may be found in **PARAPSYCHOLOGY** (p. 154).

The effects of alcohol addiction in dogs can be found in **ALCOHOL**, and in the same chapter there is a cure for premature ejaculation in the dog.

The effect of castration on dogs is mentioned in **SEX** (p. 80).

The discriminatory ability of the dog's nose is described under *Twins*.

DORSET
County of Southern England. See **SPIDERS** (p. 69).

DRAGONFLY
Useful sexual tips for female dragonflies will be found in **SEX**.

DREAMS
C. S. Hall reported in 1953 the results of a survey of the psychoanalytic literature on the interpretation of symbolism in dreams. (''A cognitive theory of dreams,'' *J. General Psychology*, 48, 169). Though admittedly nonexhaustive, his search turned up 709 different symbols in dreams. Of these, 102 were identified as symbols for the penis, making it a clear leader. In second place was the vagina, with a score of 95. These two are way ahead of the field. Other leading scores were as follows: death 62, coitus 55, masturbation 25, mother 15, father 14, breasts 13, castration 12.

DROWNING

Useful tips on drowning cats, dogs, rabbits or guinea pigs, in water or mercury, will be found in **SYNCHRONIZED DROWNING**. An effective method of drowning rats speedily will be found under *Voodoo*.

DRUGS

For the effect of hallucinogenic drugs on spiderwebs, see **SPIDERS** (pp. 66–8).

For the effect of drugs on the performance of musicians, and a discussion on the question of desirability of dope-tests at Music Festivals, see **MUSIC** (pp. 120–1).

The possible identification of drug addicts through their drawings is discussed in **BODIES** (p. 104).

The effects of cannabis on the mating habits of mice may be found in **SEX** (p. 85).

DUCKS

To find out what ducks are liable to do if you disturb them while they are copulating, turn to **SEX** (p. 81).

E

EARTHQUAKE
According to a *New York Times* report of 20 February 1977, cockroaches may be of use in predicting earthquakes. Dr. Ruth Simon, who was studying animal warnings of earthquakes, monitored the activity of cockroaches in three boxes placed in an active earthquake zone of California. Before an earthquake of small intensity, sensors in the boxes recorded a marked increase in cockroach activity. The results were described as "not conclusive but very encouraging."

ECHO-LOCATION
For a detailed explanation of how bats chirp in order to detect and pursue their prey, see *Bats*.

For an almost equally detailed explanation of how moths listen for bats' chirps in order to avoid being preyed upon, see *Moths*.

ECONOMICS
The economics of tipping in restaurants—a particularly useful guide for waitresses—will be found under *Restaurants*.

ELEPHANTS AND MARSHMALLOWS
See **HUMOR** (p. 144).

ENGINEERING
For a definitive explanation of why there are more men engineers than women engineers, see **SEX** (pp. 76–7).

ENGLAND
Anglophiles will be interested in a recent doctoral dissertation from Lund University, Sweden, entitled: "English place-names in the dative plural."

ENVIRONMENT
(This entry should be read in conjunction with *Dogs*.) Fol-

The thigh-bone of a mammoth.

lowing the initially good results obtained by depriving rats of stimulation in their formative years, variations on the theme were tried, to see how they affected the rats' abilities.

In "The Effects of Experimental Variations on Problem Solving in the Rat" (B. Hymovitch, 1952, *J. Comp. and Physiol. Psychology*), the author reports results obtained with blind rats.

"Optic enucleation was performed on one group of rats within 36 hours after their eyes opened." A second group were blinded later in life, when they were between 78 and 80 days old. Some rats of each group were then reared in a restricted environment, others were left in a free environment. As in the earlier experiment with non-blind rats, the ones with greater possibilities of stimulation and experiences as infants performed better than the others on rat intelligence tests. There was no significant difference recorded between rats blinded early or late in their developmental period.

For an account of the sexual difficulties faced by monkeys brought up in restricted environments, see **SEX** (pp. 85–7).

ERGONOMICS
The study of work; in particular of the adaptation of men, machines and environment in order to produce the most efficient results. See *Toilet Seat*.

EYE CONTACT
The unimportance of eye contact as a weapon of deception has been demonstrated in a doctoral dissertation by T.I. Mertz (Univ. of California): "Eye-gaze and hesitation as perceived indicators of deception: a field study."

In his study, 2 male and 2 female experimenters visited 20 restaurants and asked for alcoholic drinks at the bar. The experimenters were selected to look underage (less than 21). When asked their ages, the experimenters varied their behavior in specific ways involving eye contact and a possible five-second hesitation before replying. Whether they were then asked to produce identification cards was taken as a measure of perceived deception.

The author reports no significant findings. There was a trend for females to be asked for identification cards more often when they hesitated, but males were asked for cards more frequently when they did not.

One factor which may have influenced these results was the fact that in all 20 restaurants the person serving at the bar was female. The results would therefore seem to indicate that females take hesitancy in other females as a sign of dishonesty, but as a sign of honesty in males.

Taking this further, one might conjecture that women think before lying, but men do it automatically (at least when talking to women). Much more research is needed.

F

FARTING
An example of the humor inherent in farting among the Hindi-speaking children of North India may be found in **HUMOR** (p. 142).

FEAR
The effect of fear on the sexual performance of female crows and grouse will be found in **SEX** (pp. 84–5).

FISH
A great deal of information about fish is to be found in **GOLDFISH**. Their behavior under the influence of alcohol may be found in **ALCOHOL** (pp. 11–15). The entry on *Intelligence* contains further remarks on the thinking abilities of fish.

FLIES
The effect of alcohol on blowflies lacking the sense of smell is discussed in **ALCOHOL** (p. 15).

FOOD
The behavior of rats while waiting for food is discussed under *Sunflower Seeds*.

How chickens lie to other chickens about the quality of food on offer may be found in **CHICKENS** (pp. 46–7).

For preferred colors of foods, see *Orangutan*.

FOOTBALL
In *Proceedings: Sport and Science* (Edited by L. Burwitz, A. Lees, T. Reilly and R. G. Bate, 1981), a good deal is said about the potential contribution of the sports scientist to the game of Association Football. Indeed, one paper among those proceedings is even entitled: ''The potential contribution of the sports scientists to the game of Association Football.'' There does appear

A food processor.

Once the scientist has identified that central defenders should be ectomorphs and midfield players should be mesomorphs, then explained to the managers what ectomorph and mesomorph mean, there is little definite advice the scientist can give. It has been ascertained that a central defender covers an average of 7,750 meters in each game, at varying speeds, but a more detailed breakdown of this movement is needed before precise training recommendations can be made with confidence.

to be general agreement that the potential contribution is greater than the actual contribution.

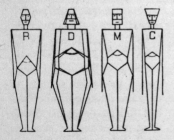

. . . central defenders should be ectomorphs, midfield players should be mesomorphs . . .

A valuable contribution was made by T. Reilly and V. Thomas in their 1976 paper "A motion analysis of work-rate in different positional roles in professional football match play" (*J. Human Movement Studies*, 2, 87–97), but perhaps the most valuable discoveries were made by J. Cohen and E. J. Dearnaley in 1962. Their paper: "Skill and Judgement of Footballers in Attempting to Score Goals" (*British J. Psychology*, 53, 71–88) was based on an analysis of the expressed confidence levels of players of differing strengths when shooting for goal. The players tested (using an interview procedure) ranged from first division professionals to occasional club players. The findings indicate that at all levels a player's confidence of scoring a goal increases the nearer he is to the enemy goal-mouth. The evidence also showed that good footballers are more confident of their goal scoring abilities than bad footballers.

FROGS

For a comparison of the mental abilities of frogs with those of lizards, crows, turtles, wolves, fish, pigeons, birds of prey, tortoises and voles, see *Intelligence*.

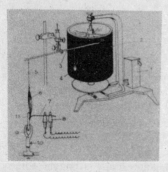

An experiment to measure the effect of an electric current on the muscle (6) of a frog's leg.

FRUIT FLIES

A failure to demonstrate that fruit flies have psychokinetic powers is recorded in **PARA-PSYCHOLOGY** (p. 154). Perhaps their lack of psychokinetic powers helps explain why so many fruit flies get caught and eaten by bats. For a rather tedious account of how bats catch fruit flies, and how to estimate how many of them have been caught, see *Bats*.

FUNERAL

One of the categories in the Taxonomy of Death Jokes (see **HUMOR** p. 135) and the only one of those categories which is an anagram of ''real fun.''

A reference to the question of whether a man can witness his own funeral may be found in **PARAPSYCHOLOGY** (p. 157).

G

GASTRIC ULCER

According to W. L. Sawrey and J. D. Weisz ("An Experimental Method of Producing Gastric Ulcers," *J. Comp. and Physiol. Psych.* 1956, 49, 269–70) a conflict between the separate drives of fear and hunger can result in the formation of gastric ulcers in rats.

Their experimental design was to have rats in a box with food and water at one end of the box and a grid, which could be electrified, nearby. While the electricity was turned on, the rats could not approach the food without suffering shocks. The electricity was left on all the time, except for 1 hour every 2 days. The rats were left in this state for 30 days. Another group of rats, acting as controls, were in a similar box, but with no electric shocks. For them, food was also made available only for 1 hour in every 48. So each group had the same eating opportunities, but the experimental group had constant temptation and electric shocks too.

The experimental group subsequently developed gastric ulcers.

GEGBE

A West African language of the Kwa group with a lot to be said for its predicate phrases. See *Grammar*.

GELOTOSCOPY

The art of divining the future, or making character readings, from the quality of a person's laughter is properly termed gelotoscopy (though some writers have preferred the etymologically dubious geloscopy). Little research on this topic appears to have been carried out recently, leaving the Abbé Domascere's 1561 pronouncements unchallenged. (See **HUMOR** p. 139).

GENITAL SURGERY
See *Bees*.

GENITAL SIZE
A helpful guide towards interpreting the humor of references to genital size in dirty jokes will be found in **HUMOR** (p. 140).

GERBIL
A recent discussion of the sounds made by young gerbils will be found in: McCauley, P.J. and Elwood, R.W. (1984): "Hunger and the Vocalisation of Infant Gerbils," *Dev. Psychobiol.* 17.

Infant gerbils were deprived of food by removing their mother from the cage for 3 hours on alternate days. In order to take account of the influence of parental affection, a control group had their fathers removed for similar time periods. The sounds emitted by the gerbils were analysed, but no significant differences between the 2 groups were discovered. The experimental group (deprived of food), however, were found to have lost weight. The researchers conclude that gerbils have an absence of mode of communicating a nutritional state.

This means that gerbils don't have a word for "hungry."

Tips on feeding gerbils will be found in **PARAPSYCHOLOGY** (p. 96), where also is discussed the fascinating question of whether man, by willpower alone, can influence the activity level of gerbils.

GERMANY
For a brief discussion of the behavior of American and German pigeons as compared with Cambridge pigeons, see *Pigeons*.

GIBBONS
The singing habits of gibbons will be found in **MUSIC** (p. 120), though sadly there is no reference to whether their repertoires contain anything composed by Orlando Gibbons (1583–1625). One would conjecture not.

GOATS
The effects of exhibitionism, voyeurism and bondage on the sexual activity of goats is discussed in **SEX**.

GOLDFISH
For a discussion of the telepathic or psychokinetic pow-

ers of goldfish, see **PARA-PSYCHOLOGY** (p. 151).

For a detailed account of the effects of alcohol on the learning abilities and memory of goldfish, and how they fall over when drunk and whether goldfish have hangovers, see **ALCOHOL** (pp. 11–15).

For everything else about goldfish, see **GOLDFISH**.

GOLF

The Scottish parliament passed a law in 1457 which decreed that ''goff be utterly cryit doune and not usit.'' This typically small-minded bureaucratic approach to science must have severely hindered research on golf. In fact we had to wait until 1984 for a doctoral thesis by K. R. Campbell of the Univ. of Illinois: ''Application of Optimal Control Theory to Human Movement Problems: The Golf Swing'' before a proper theoretical basis was established for the game.

This thesis developed a three-link model of the golf swing, with upper torso, left arm and club as the segments. The torques acting on torso, left shoulder and left wrist were identified as the system controls. An inverse dynamic analysis using two-dimensional cinematographic techniques was employed to examine the validity of the model. (I think this means that they took films of golfers.) In order to obtain data about the position, velocity and torque at shoulder and wrist, an iso-kinetic strength testing device was used. These data were subsequently submitted to a stepwise multiple regression analysis. The optimal solutions were found to provide valuable insight into the mechanics of the golf drive.

GRAMMAR

For the dative plural, see *England*.

For predicate phrases, however, the reader is referred to a doctoral thesis by E. Jondoh of Indiana University in 1980: ''Some Aspects of the Predicate Phrase in Gegbe.'' (For anyone whose knowledge of West African languages may be rusty, we take this opportunity to remind you that Gegbe is a language of the Kwa group.) We assume from the title of this thesis that we may look forward to ''Further Aspects of the Predicate Phrase in Gegbe,'' and perhaps even an eventual definitive work on the subject. Whether Gegbe itself has a word or expression to mean ''predicate phrase'' is a matter open to conjecture.

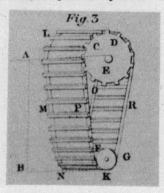

A useful device for moving capital letters around.

GRAVITY
For the effects of gravity upon mice, see *Mouse*.

For the effects of gravity upon cats, see *Diving*.

For the effects of gravity upon toilet paper, see *Toilet tissue*.

GREAT CRESTED FLY-CATCHER
For a lurid account of miscegenation by a great crested fly-catcher, see **COURTSHIP** (p. 91).

GROUSE
For full instructions on how to ruffle a ruffled grouse, see **SEX** (p. 84).

GUINEA PIG
It was R. F. Becker and W. Donnell who investigated in 1952 (*J. Comp. and Physiol. Psych.*) what effect it has on a guinea pig if you strangle it at birth. In fact, they strangled their guinea pigs just prenatally, reporting the results in a paper entitled: ''Learning Behaviour in Guinea Pigs Subjected to Asphyxia at Birth.''

Guinea pigs were asphyxiated in utero by attaching clamps to the uterine vessels near the term of pregnancy. One animal in each litter was delivered by Caesarean, without having been asphyxiated, to act as a control. Of the asphyxiated guinea pigs, one group were subjected to a brief stifling, then allowed to breathe spontaneously. A second group were asphyxiated until they were comatose then revived with drugs.

They were all then allowed to grow up without being further molested, until they were old enough to be given a learning task. Compared with the control guinea pigs, those from group one were found to be hesitant and slow learners; group two, however, were just plain stupid. Two weeks later, after being given time to forget their lessons, all the guinea pigs were tested again. The control animals had remembered well, but all the experimental animals needed retraining.

In view of these findings, pet guinea pig owners would be well advised, if they don't want their guinea pigs to grow up stupid, not to clamp the uterine vessels of the mother guinea pigs during pregnancy.

An easier way to kill guinea pigs will be found in **SYNCHRONIZED DROWNING** (p. 31).

Castrated guinea pigs will be found in **SEX** (p. 80).

GULL
For an account of the laughing gull as mugger, see **Kleptoparasitism**.

H

HALLUCINATION
For a discussion of alcohol-induced hallucinations in dogs, see **ALCOHOL** (p. 8)

The effect of hallucinogens on the web building of spiders may be found in **SPIDERS** (pp. 65-8), where also is described the effect on spiders of drinking the urine of psychiatric patients who are suffering from hallucinations.

HAMSTER
The effect of castration on the sexual behavior of the male hamster is mentioned in **SEX** (p. 81).

HAND-SHAKING
The role of the handshake in American culture was the subject of a 1984 dissertation at Boston University by P. E. Webster. Entitled "An Ethnographic Study of Handshaking," its intention was to identify the function of the greeting handshake. The results indicated that there are, in fact, several functions of the handshake: to seal identification and provide access in initial encounters; to communicate solidarity and bonding in subsequent encounters; and to communicate relative status and subjective personal information. Most importantly, the writer concluded that handshaking is a complex nonverbal form of behavior.

Thanks to this research, we may all now shake hands in fuller knowledge of what we are doing.

HAWAII
For a full description of how sharks mate in the waters off Hawaii, see **SEX** (p. 81).

For a connection between coffee, alcohol and heart disease among Japanese men living in Hawaii, see **ALCOHOL** (pp. 19-20).

Modern psychology rarely
approaches the mathematical
precision attained by the
old physiognomists.

HEAD
To discover what to do with
your head while dancing in
Tonga, see **MUSIC** (p. 125).

For an estimate of the risk
of head damage to dragonflies
while mating, see **SEX** (p.
81).

For an account of where
sharks put their heads while
mating, see **SEX** (p. 81).

For an account of the aph-
rodisiac value of a severed turkey head to another young turkey, see **SEX** (p. 84).

HEADACHE
(Not tonight, I've got a)
   See **COURTSHIP** (pp. 97–
8).

HEADLESSNESS
For the effect of decerebration
on chickens, see **CHICKEN**
(p. 40).

HEADS (MULTIPLE)
For an experimental verifica-
tion of the principle that two
heads are better than one, see
WORMS (p. 55).

HEDGEHOG
According to research by H.
Walhovd in 1984 ("Breeding
habits of the European hedgehog in Denmark," *Z. Saeu-
getierkd.*, 49) the average
family size of Danish hedge-
hogs is 4.75. They mate between late July and early
September and have one litter
at most each year.

HINDEMITH
(Paul, 1895–1963). Com-
poser, fancied by the discriminating pigeon. See **MUSIC**
(p. 118).

HOLES

According to a paper in *Nature* (1964, Vol. 203, p. 792) entitled: "Apparent size of holes felt with the tongue," an illusion in the size of a hole is found, when felt by the tongue, if the hole is between an eighth and a quarter of an inch thick, but for holes between three-eighths and seven-sixteenths of an inch, no illusion in size is felt.

This finding would appear to be of greatest importance to people who earn their livings estimating sizes of holes by feeling them with their tongues, though the full range of potential applications is doubtless much wider.

HOLLAND

For a reference to Dutch Homosexuals, see **SEX** (p. 85).

HOMICIDE

The lighter side of homicide, how to find the laughter in manslaughter, may be found in **HUMOR** (p. 135).

HOMOSEXUALITY

For an indication of the amount of alcohol required in order to accomplish a successful homosexual seduction, see **ALCOHOL** (p. 16).

For a discussion of homosexuality in mice, pigs and Dutchmen, see **SEX** (p. 85).

The question of whether ho-

Recerebration is a bigger problem . . .

mosexuals of either gender betray their sexual preferences in their drawings of people is discussed in **BODIES** (p. 103).

onstrates the distinction between a "humor rating" and a "mirth response." Whereas one's objective assessment of the funniness of a joke (the humor rating) may stay relatively stable on repetition of the joke, one's mirth response (as measured by the laughter evoked by the joke) tends to decrease with repetition.

The subject of mirth and humor is dealt with extensively in **HUMOR**.

The more specific topic of Jewish humor will be found under *Judaism*.

HORSE
A comment on horse sense will be found under *Intelligence*.

HUMOR
Stop me if you've heard this one before, but research has shown that jokes are liable to be perceived as less funny if you have heard them before. A recent study by I. Gavanski (1986) entitled "Differential sensitivity of humour ratings and mirth responses to cognitive and affective components of the humour response" (*J. Personal and Social Psychology*, 51, 209–14) clearly dem-

Improving the horsepower of a machine with more hay.

HUNGER
An affective state often char-

acterized by prior lack of food. A discussion of the young gerbil's lack of vocal response to hunger may be found under *Gerbil*. The role of the hunger drive in producing gastric ulcers in rats may be found under *Gastric ulcer*.

I

ICELAND
The possible influence of mushrooms in early Icelandic history may be found under *Mushroom*.

IMBECILE
See *Intelligence*.

INCEST
A discussion of the increased difficulty in seducing one's relatives is found in **ALCOHOL** (p. 16).

INFIDELITY
The appropriateness of rats as an animal model of human infidelity is discussed in **COURTSHIP** (pp. 94–6), where also will be found some disturbing information about the high incidence of infidelity among pied and collared flycatchers.

INFORMATION TECHNOLOGY
The Proceedings of the Third International Theriological Congress (1982) contains an interesting paper by Frank and Frank on "Information Processing in Dogs and Wolves." It is an account of an experiment designed to test a 1980 theory of Frank. The theoretical model advances hypotheses that wolves should be better than dogs at complex problem-solving tasks, but that dogs, because of their many generations of domestication, should be better at tasks that involve preliminary training.

Four eastern wolf pups and 4 Alaskan malamute pups were all reared identically from birth, then at a suitable stage in their development given a series of tasks to perform. Seven of the tasks involved a large element of training; seven further needed no training to perform, but involved only problem-solving abilities.

The dogs cheated by telling one another the answers.

The dogs did better than the wolves on 5 of the 7 training tasks, but the wolves outperformed the dogs on all 7 of the problem-solving tasks. The results thus confirmed the hypotheses, and may help to explain why the Drug Squad does not employ sniffer-wolves.

INHIBITION
Inhibited fish are referred to in **GOLDFISH** (p. 27).

INTELLIGENCE
A great deal of research has been carried out on the topic of intelligence, including a study which has been going on for more than 25 years by L. V. Krushinsky at Moscow University. The aim of the project is a comparative study of the elemental reasoning abilities of different species of animal. One of the basic tests involves an opaque screen which separates an animal from a food bowl. There are 3 holes in the screen, through which the animal may poke its head and reach the food. The food bowl is made to slide away from the animal while it eats, and the question is whether the animal has the wit to withdraw its head, move in the direction of movement of the bowl, and poke its head through the next hole for another bite of food.

A wide variety of animals have been tested on this experiment and the results give a league table of brightness. Mammals are found to be not invariably better than birds or reptiles. Lizards, crows, turtles and wolves do best; fish, frogs, pigeons and voles do worst. Birds of prey perform worse than pigeons. Herbivorous and carnivorous tortoises are both good at it. (A longer discussion by J. Crocker can be found in the *New Scientist*, 10th October issue, 1985.)

Animal intelligence in action.

An account of animal intelligence on a more difficult task may be found in Warren, J. M. and Warren, H. B. (1962). ''Reversal Learning by Horse and Raccoon,'' *J. Genetic Psychology*, 100, 215–20. The design here involved confusing the animal, by first teaching it to discriminate between two possible choices, then reversing the conditions so that it had to learn to make the previously incorrect choice. (A similar reversal experiment performed on inebriated goldfish will be found in **ALCOHOL** pp. 13–14).

The confusion is increased by again reversing the condition every time the animal has learned to get it right. When this is tried on rats and cats, they show a progressive reduction in the number of errors made on each reversal, before they get the hang of it again. What Warren and Warren did was to show that the two horses and one raccoon used in their experiment also show a rapid reduction in errors. They also mention that qualitatively similar results have been obtained in comparable experiments with cats, human imbeciles and rats.

Putting all the results together shows that rats and imbeciles are the quickest, cats

Hyper intelligent chimp prepares for a long pot of the blue into the corner pocket.

and raccoons slowest. Unlike the simpler task referred to in the Moscow work above, the reversal task does clearly differentiate between higher vertebrates on the one hand and fish and invertebrates on the other. Chickens are good at it, but it is generally too difficult for fish, crabs and woodlice.

Incidentally, if you need to know how to teach a raccoon something, the answer is to reward it with pork kidney.

IRRATIONAL FEAR

Irrational fears in dogs are referred to in **SYNCHRONIZED DROWNING** (p. 35).

A monkey showing intelligence and a working knowledge of German (Ziel = goal).

J

JAPAN
The rhythmic abilities of the Japanese are discussed in **MUSIC** (p. 123).

Their drinking habits and heart problems on moving to Hawaii are referred to in **ALCOHOL** (pp. 19–20).

JAZZ
The effect of playing jazz to cheetahs and monkeys is referred to in **MUSIC** (p. 118).

JUDAISM
The musical abilities of Jewish children are investigated in **MUSIC** (p. 123), but far more interesting is the question of the Jewish sense of humor. L. Weller, E. Amitsour, and R. Pazzi in 1976 ("Reaction to absurd humour by Jews of eastern and western descent," *J. Social Psychology*, 98, 159–63) hypothesized that Israeli Jews of eastern descent would find absurd jokes less funny than would Israeli Jews of western descent. This was based upon a theory that the humor of absurdity stems from the need for release from rational logic. Since western culture lays a stronger emphasis on rationality, people from western backgrounds should feel a greater need for the release offered by absurd jokes.

So eastern and western Jews were told absurd jokes, then asked to rate them and explain why they found them funny (if indeed they did).

The findings confirmed the hypothesis, showing that western Israeli Jews are more likely than eastern Israeli Jews to enjoy absurd jokes. How this particular finding fits into a general theory of Jewish humor appreciation must await a longer and more detailed study.

K

KLEPTO-PARASITISM
Basically this is an up-market word for mugging. An excellent account of pelicans being mugged by gulls is given by Carroll, S. P. and Cramer, K. L. (1985): "Age differences in klepto-parasitism by laughing gulls (*Larus atricilla*) on adult and juvenile brown pelicans (*Pelicanus occidentalis*)," *Animal Behaviour*, 85, 201–5.

Their findings are based on observations of gulls stealing fish from pelicans. Whereas young gulls tend to select their victims at random, adult gulls are observed to steal more often from juvenile pelicans. It was also observed that when being mugged by gulls, juvenile pelicans attempt evasion less frequently than adult pelicans. On the other hand, adult pelicans are more likely to be good victims for the gull, since they are better foragers and are therefore more likely to have fish. Whether the adult gulls have the right strategy is therefore still an open question.

KNOWLEDGE
A theory of the molecular basis for knowledge storage and retrieval, and in particular whether knowledge is edible, is discussed in **WORMS**.

L

LATVIA
The problem of classifying Latvian folk music is discussed in **MUSIC** (pp. 126–8).

LAUGHTER
A behavioral response to humor, but rather unreliable as a guide to an objective humor-rating of the laughter-provoking stimulus. See **HUMOR** (pp. 139–40). See also *Humor* for an interesting observation on the distinction between mirth and humor.

LEG
A limb which has aroused a great deal of interest among researchers in a wide range of different fields.

For a discussion of the leg-movements of stick insects, see *Stick insect*.

For a reference to the sensitivity of the leg to a sugar, see *Butterfly*.

An account of an experiment to determine the contribution of the legs towards aquatic motion will be found under *Swimming*.

What to do with your legs while dancing in Tonga will be found in **MUSIC** (p. 125).

How the loss of a leg or two affects the web building of spiders will be found in **SPIDERS** (pp. 64–5).

Attitudes towards legs and the effect of legs on self-esteem will be found in **BODIES** (p. 108).

LIBRARIANSHIP
The relationship between innovating processes and the effectiveness of selected innovations in university libraries in Nigeria is discussed in a 1984 Michigan University doctoral thesis of that title by M. G. Ochogwu. He mentions that scholarly attention has been given only in the last decade to the introduction of innovations in libraries. His

research revealed that while a good deal of innovation was going on in university libraries in Nigeria, most of the library staff were not well-informed about the innovations selected for this particular study.

LITERATURE

The extent of the degradation of British publishing was revealed in a 1964 paper by W. P. Brown (*British Journal of Psychology* 55, 365–8) entitled: "The titles of paperback books." A number of books were selected for the study, all of whose titles in paperback differed from the original hardback editions. Subjects were asked to rate the book titles on a number of different scales to assess the impact and connotations of the titles, as well as their accuracy in describing the book itself. In most cases the new paperback title was rated lower on evaluation and/or higher on potency. "The change of title is seen as an attempt to increase 'package appeal' of the book, perhaps by enhancing its capacity to hold the attention of the prospective purchaser."

LIZARD

Most female lizards are indiscriminate in their choice of male lizards. This important finding was reported (*J. Herpetology*, vol. 19, No. 2) in 1985 by R. M. Andrews in a paper: "Mate choice by females of the lizard, *Anolis carolinensis*."

Female lizards were given a number of males with whom they might mate. Only one-third of the females tested showed a significant tendency to prefer one or two particular males. The other two-thirds of the female lizards were reported to associate with males randomly.

When females did show preference for one particular male over another, the findings indicated that the relative size of the males was not an important factor in determining her choice.

Since we know how bright lizards can be (see *Intelligence*) these results are not to be lightly discounted.

The effect of barometric pressure and humidity on the psychokinetic abilities of lizards is mentioned in **PARAPSYCHOLOGY** (p. 152).

ZOOLOGICAL SOCIETY OF LONDON.

LIST OF DUPLICATE ANIMALS

IN THE

GARDENS FOR SALE.

OCTOBER, 1876.

MAMMALS.

		£	s.	d.
2	Collared Fruit Bats, male and female (Cynonycteris collaris)...	8	o	o
1	Ocelot, male (Felis pardalis)	4	o	o
1	African Civet (Viverra civetta)	3	10	o
2	Grey Ichneumons (Herpestes griseus) ... ...each	1	10	o
2	Marsh Ichneumons (Herpestes paludosus) ... ...each	1	10	o
2	Common Foxes, male and female (Canis vulpes) ... ...each	1	10	o
1	Pine Marten (Martes abietum)	2	o	o
1	Tayra, male (Galictis barbara)	6	o	o
2	Common Raccoons (Procyon lotor) ... ...each	2	o	o
1	Coati (Nasua nasica)	1	10	o
1	Kinkajou (Cercoleptes caudivolvulus)	4	o	o
2	Chinchillas, male and female (Chinchilla lanigera) ... the pair	5	c	o
2	Hairy-rumped Agoutis (Dasyprocta prymnolopha) ... ...each	2	o	o
2	Central American Agoutis (Dasyprocta punctata) ... ...each	2	o	o
2	Wild Boars, male and female (Sus scrofa—adult) ... the pair	15	o	o
1	Eland, female (Oreas canna)	50	o	o
1	Three-quarter bred Zebu, female (Bred between Bos indicus and B. frontalis—born Jan. 5, 1875)	20	o	o
1	Three-quarter Bred Zebu, female (Ditto ditto, born March 11, 1876)	20	o	o
1	Wapiti Deer, female (Cervus canadensis—born Sept. 18, 1875)	25	o	o
1	Molucca Deer, male (Cervus moluccensis—born May 19, 1875)	5	o	o
1	Molucca Deer, male (Cervus moluccensis—born April 23, 1876)	5	o	o
1	Axis Deer, male (Cervus axis)	8	o	o
1	Reeve's Muntjac, female (Cervulus Reevesi)...	4	o	o
1	Sclater's Muntjac, male (Cervulus Sclateri)	10	o	o
3	Vulpine Phalangers (Phalangista vulpina) ... ...each	1	5	o
1	Great Kangaroo, male (Macropus giganteus)	25	o	o
2	Hybrid Rat Kangaroos (Bred between Hypsiprymnus ogylbi and H. gaimardi) ... ...each	2	o	o

M

MACAQUE MONKEY
(From the Portuguese, *macaco*, a monkey). The macaque monkey is believed to be the first nonhuman mammal in which female orgasm has been identified. See *Orgasm*.

"Jazz is not for me, I fear."

MARIHUANA
A drug known to have effects on the webbuilding of spiders. See **SPIDERS** (p.64).

MATING
There's a great deal of this going on in **SEX** and **COURTSHIP**, but see also **GOLDFISH** (p. 25) for the effect of noselessness on mating, and *Lizard* for even more information on the subject.

MEMORY
A theory of how memory might, but almost certainly doesn't, work will be found in **WORMS** (p. 51). Further influential results on memory will be found under **ALCOHOL** (pp. 11–5).

MONGOLISM
An investigation into the musical ability of Mongol chil-

dren is reported in **MUSIC** (p. 123).

MONKEY
The effect of jazz on monkeys is reported in **MUSIC** (p. 118). The question of whether female monkeys have orgasms is thoroughly explored under *Orgasm*.

MONOGAMY
A theory of the reasons for monogamy in sparrows is found in **COURTSHIP** (p. 94).

MOON
Whether rats' precognition of death is affected by the moon phase is a topic mentioned in **PARAPSYCHOLOGY** (p. 154).

MOSQUITO
Insect much favored as bat food. See *Bat*.

MOTH
The moth is another thing (cf. *Mosquito*) that bats would like to eat, but moths are better at eluding bats. K. D. Roeder and A. E. Treat ("The detection and evasion of bats by moths," *American Scientist*, 49, 135–48) described in 1961 how they do it.

Their experiments revealed that several families of moths have evolved ultrasonic "ears" near their waists, which can detect the high frequency chirps of bats. The functioning of these ears (actually tympanic membranes) was investigated by implanting a fine metal electrode under the tympanic nerve in order to eavesdrop on reports to the moth's nervous system. "The insect subject was pinned on cork so that one of its ears had an unrestricted sound field, and with the help of a microscope its tympanic nerve was exposed and placed on electrodes." Both artificial sounds and bat sounds were used to demonstrate the efficiency of the moth ear as a bat detector. When properly stimulated by bat sounds, the moth begins to adopt erratic flight patterns. (Presumably the moth had been unpinned from the cork when this last fact was discovered.) The net result is that fewer moths get eaten by bats.

MOTIVATION
See *Stickleback*.

MOUSE

Drunkenness in mice is a serious problem which is discussed on p. 8 of **ALCOHOL**. To what extent the inebriate behavior of the mouse may be due to its genetic makeup may be found in the same chapter on p. 16.

The sexual, and more specifically ejaculatory, behavior of castrated male mice is discussed in detail in **SEX** (p. 80).

The paranormal abilities of mice to avoid random electric shocks will be found in **PARAPSYCHOLOGY** (p. 150).

What happens when you drop a mouse onto a hard surface was described by M. R. A. Chance in 1953 (*British J. Animal Behaviour*, i. 118–9) in his paper: ''The posture of a falling mouse.''

In his experiments, mice were dropped 10 feet and their postures photographed. They were found to fall with jaws partially open, and their heads held with the snout 10° to 15° above the horizontal.

The effectiveness of this posture in saving them from injury was further ascertained by dropping 10 male mice onto a hard surface. But 5 of the mice had been anesthetized before being dropped, so did not adopt their natural falling posture.

One hour later, both groups of mice were killed and examined for hemorrhage caused by the fall. The experiment was spoiled a little by one of the anesthetized mice, which had already died of its injuries within an hour of the fall. There were, however, still enough injuries (mainly internal) among the other 4 anesthetized mice, but only one small injury among the 5 which were conscious when dropped.

We may thus conclude that when falling, a mouse adopts a posture designed to protect it from injury on landing.

MOUSTACHE

The effect of a false moustache on chickens and woodpeckers is discussed in **CHICKENS** (pp. 40–2).

MOZART

(Wolgang Amadeus, 1756–91). Several Mozartian themes are discussed in **MUSIC** (pp. 128–30).

MUSHROOM

The role of the mushroom in Siberian and early Icelandic history is discussed by H. D. Fabing's 1956 paper: "On Going Berserk: A neurochemical inquiry" (*American J. Psychology*, November 1956).

The original Berserk was a probably mythical warrior who refused to don armor when going into battle, preferring to fight in a bear-skin (*ber-serk*). Later in Icelandic history, around the time of the sagas (870–1030 A.D.) and perhaps before, predatory groups of brawlers and killers roamed around, creating havoc wherever they appeared. They were known as Berserks, and were famed and feared for their acts of wild strength. According to Fabing:

"There is a fascinating theory that Berserksgang, or the act of 'going beserk' may not have been a psychogenically determined habit pattern, but may rather have been due to the eating of toxic mushrooms."

He compares the reported behavior of the Berserks with that of some Siberian tribes of the Kamchatka peninsula, where mushrooms are eaten for their hallucinogenic properties. The mushroom, *Amanita muscaria*, contains a substance called n-n-dimethyl serotonin which produces hallucinations. In fact, the drug may be found still in some quantity in the urine of those who have eaten such mushrooms. It is reported that the Siberian, drunk on mushrooms, will drink his own urine in order to prolong the hallucinations—or he may offer it to others as a treat. It is further reported that such urine can be drunk successively by 5 people, and all will gain the hallucinogenic effect.

(We await with interest laboratory tests to confirm this last finding).

To add further weight to this theory, there are similar accounts of Mexicans who consider sacred another type of mushroom containing the same drug. Fabing's conclusion is that "the famed fury of the Berserks was what we would call a model psychosis today."

MUSIC
(Including Musicology and Ethnomusicology). See **MU-SIC**.

N

NARCISSISM

A good deal about self-esteem will be found in **BODIES**, but a further result on the effects of sex differences on narcissistic response is worth reporting here.

R. M. Zeitner and D. G. Weight examined in 1979 what happened to the pupils of people's eyes when they looked at photographs of themselves. ("The pupillometric response as a parameter of self-esteem", *J. Clinical Psychology*, 35, 176–83.)

Previous work had established a correlation between interest in a stimulus and dilatation of the pupils. It was therefore hypothesized that a person's self-esteem would correspond with how much his pupils dilated when looking at a photograph of himself. 49 females and 33 males were therefore enlisted to look at their own photographs and have their pupils measured. They were also assessed on an independent measure of self-esteem.

The results for the males showed no correlation whatsoever between pupil dilatation and self-esteem. The females did show a correlation, but in the opposite direction from that predicted: the less they liked themselves, the more their eyes widened.

By way of explanation, the researchers offer a theory that in a situation with implicit anxiety states, the sympathetic nervous system predominates over the interest value of a stimulus. Females may be constitutionally more prone than males to exhibit such a sympathetic reaction, or they may be more responsive to the body-image properties inherent in photographs.

Or the whole experiment may have been a bit of a washout.

Please ignore this illustration. He is only trying to draw attention to himself.

NECROPHILIA

For an account of an attempt at experimentally induced necrophilia among poultry, see **CHICKENS** (pp. 42–3).

For the more amusing side of necrophilia, see **HUMOR** (p. 135).

NEUROSIS

For the effect of alcohol on neurotic dogs, see **ALCOHOL** (p. 9).

For a reference to the effect of alcohol on neurotic cats, see **ALCOHOL** (p. 10).

NEW YORK

The sexual fidelity of New York sparrows is discussed in **COURTSHIP** (p. 94).

NEWT

The fickleness of the male newt is exposed in **COURTSHIP** (pp. 93–4).

NIGERIA

See *Librarianship*.

NIPPLE ATTACHMENT

The effect of prenatal doses of alcohol on an infant rat's period of attachment to its mother's nipple may be found in **ALCOHOL** (p. 15).

NITRATE PATCH

Several interesting side effects of the misuse of a nitrate patch may be found in **COURTSHIP** (pp. 97–8).

NUMERACY

The question of whether rats are numerate is one which has attracted a good deal of interest in recent years. In their paper: ''Autocontingencies: Rats count to three to predict safety from shock'' (*Animal LearningBehaviour*, vol 11, No. 1, February 1983), H. Davis and J. Memmott end with the words:

. . . The authors conclude that rats may be taught to count, but such behaviour is highly unnatural and may be blocked or overshadowed by more salient sources of information.

A few months later (November 1983), in the same journal, there appeared a paper entitled: ''Can a rat count?'', by H. Imada, H. Shuku and M. Noriya, who concluded:

. . . There was no evidence that rats could count under either signalled or unsignalled conditions.

The current state of knowledge would therefore appear to be that Japanese rats cannot count, and that other rats might be able to, but only with difficulty.

O

OCTOPUS
See **GOLDFISH** (pp. 24–5).

OPIUM
A reference to opium as part of a treatment for premature ejaculation will be found in **SEX** (p. 73).

OPTICAL ILLUSION
The reaction of goldfish to optical illusions will be found in **GOLDFISH** (p. 23).

ORANGUTAN
You may frequently have wondered what color food orangutans like best. Some progress towards the answer is to be found in a 1985 paper by R. B. Barbiers (*Zoo Biol* vol. 4, No. 3) entitled: "Orang-utans' colour preference for food items."

Three adult and 3 juvenile orangutans were offered items of food artificially colored red, green, blue and orange. It was found that the juveniles ate more colored food than the adults, but the adults ate more quickly. One of the juveniles showed a distinct liking for red food.

More research is clearly needed.

ORGASM

For a case of paroxysmal sneezing following orgasm, see **COURTSHIP** (p. 98).

An early diagnosis and cure for the malady of female orgasm will be found in **SEX** (p. 75). This reference, however, only discusses human orgasms. The question of orgasms in female nonhumans has been a matter of some recent debate.

According to Dr. Lynda Birke, writing in the *New Scientist* in December 1986, orgasmic responses have been claimed to have been induced in female rats in the following manner:

> The female was grasped by placing the thumb and ring finger anterior to the iliac crests and the index and third finger on opposite sides of the tail so that their tips palpated the vulvar area.

These results were open to dispute, because although there was a good deal of heavy breathing and squeaking from the rats, the full physiological measurements needed to demonstrate a definite orgasm were not taken.

Fred Burton, at the International Congress of Primatology in 1971, obtained orgasmic responses in female rhesus monkeys. The animals were restrained and their genitals mechanically stimulated.

One animal bit the experimenter.

Fast heart rates and increased blood flow to the genitals were measured. One animal bit the experimenter.

Among other primates, it has been noted that female chacma baboons indulge in staccato grunting, while rhesus monkey females are liable at moments of passion to reach back and clutch their partner. But is it a real orgasm?

To answer this climactic

question, researchers in Rotterdam selected from a group of stump-tailed macaque monkeys the female who was apparently most orgasmic. Radio transmitters were implanted under her skin to monitor heart rate and to measure the force of her uterine contractions. During a sexual encounter (presumably with another monkey), she experienced a fifty-second series of uterine contractions, during which her heart rate rose from 186 to 210 per minute. Her mouth adopted a rounded shape and she emitted repeated vocalizations. The conclusion is that female monkeys do have orgasms.

P

PARAPSYCHOLOGY
The science of the unscientific. See **PARAPSYCHOLOGY**.

PELICAN
Hapless, and frequently fishless, victim of marauding gulls. For further explanation see *Klepto-parasitism*.

PENILE TUMESCENCE
A reliable guide to sexual arousal in males (see **ALCOHOL** p. 16). If you're looking for a tool to enable you to hear expansion occurring in a penis, see **SEX** (p. 87).

PENIS
For the effects of surgery on the male genitalia of bees, see *Bees*.

For a comment upon the penis of the dog, see **SYNCHRONIZED DROWNING** (p. 35).

The penis as front-runner in the league of psychoanalytic dream symbols will be found under *Dreams*.

To discover why the possession of a penis is thought to make boys better than girls at experimental sciences and mathematics, turn to **SEX** (p. 77).

PET
For the characteristics of dog and cat owners, see **SYNCHRONIZED DROWNING** (p. 34).

For the characteristics of a pet cat, owned by a parapsychologist, see **PARAPSYCHOLOGY** (p. 152).

For the effect of domestication on the songs of pet canaries, see **MUSIC** (p. 119).

PHEROMONES
The role played by pheromones in influencing the mating behavior of goldfish may

218

be found in **GOLDFISH** (p. 25).

The role played by pheromones in influencing the mating behavior of spiders may be found in **SPIDERS** (p. 61).

PHILODENDRA
Whether the philodendron leaf is sufficiently sensitive to be able to predict the death of a nearby shrimp is a matter which has concerned parapsychologists for some time. See **PARAPSYCHOLOGY** (pp. 154–6).

PHOTOGRAPHY
See *Narcissism*.

PHYSICS
For a purely physical explanation of why boy physicists are better than girl physicists, see **SEX** (p. 77).

PICTISH
Pertaining to the Picts, or their language. See **MUSIC** (p. 126).

PIGS
For the effect of loud music on the sexual orientation and hearing ability of pigs, see **SEX** (p. 85).

PIGEON
The homing abilities of pigeons have attracted a good deal of research. One of the best recent contributions has been that of G. V. T. Matthews in 1963 (*Animal Behaviour*, 11, 310–17) in a paper entitled: ''The orientation of pigeons as affected by the learning of landmarks and by the distance of displacement.''

To examine how their homing instincts worked, 30 Cambridge-educated pigeons were released at various distances from home. Up to a distance of 18 miles, it was clear that they navigated their return journeys by using landmarks which they could recognize. Between 50 and 79 miles, and even further, they showed an ability to orientate themselves immediately in the right direction for flying home. When released between 23 and 35 miles from home, however, they showed no particular orientation, but flew apparently at random until either close enough to use landmarks, or far enough away for their orientating abilities to come into action.

German and American pigeons have been observed to show another type of behavior. They have shown a tendency to fly north at first, wherever they are released. This is similar to the behavior of mallards, which also seem to have a favorite direction in which to fly, though different strains of mallard have different characteristic directions.

It may also be interesting to compare the poor performance of pigeons on intelligence tests (see *Intelligence*) with their discrimination when it comes to listening to classical music (see **MUSIC** pp. 118-9).

POLAR BEAR

No justice can be done to the subject of polar bears without full acknowledgement to the marvellous paper by T. J. Oleson, ''Polar Bears in the Middle Ages'' (*Canadian History Review*, 1950, 47-55). The interested reader is strongly advised to hunt down a copy of this paper for himself. Here, as a totally inadequate tribute, are the closing lines:

> Mediaeval man—contrary to what is often believed—was filled with an insatiable curiosity, though he did not as scrupulously as modern man commit his learning and his ignorance to paper. Yet he committed more than is yet realized. When the richest of all mines—the fifteenth century—has been worked and reworked, it will be found that he knew more than we think. His knowledge of the Arctic regions of America will be one of those revelations. To that knowledge the polar bear made his not insignificant contribution.

PONY

For an interesting example of a white pony, painted sometimes purple and sometimes with black and purple spots, see *Taxidermy*.

PORNOGRAPHY

In 1976, the *Journal of Social Psychology* (vol 98, 235–45) published the results of an investigation by M. Brown, D. M. Amoroso and E. E. Ware, entitled: "The behavioral effects of viewing pornography." Their research had involved showing pornographic slides to 56 male college students, asking for their reactions, then monitoring their subsequent sexual activity and comparing it with their normal level. *"The activities of major interest were masturbation, petting, coitus and sexual dreams."*

Reported results included the following:

77% of the subjects described the slide viewing as enjoyable.

67% said they wanted to see more.

52% reported being sexually aroused.

21% were disgusted.

9% were shocked.

6% said they wanted to leave.

When asked whether the slides showed any activities that were new to them and which they would like to try, 29% replied yes.

About half of the subjects reported masturbation, petting and sex dreams at least once in the week before viewing; about a quarter of the subjects reported coitus. These figures were very similar during the week after viewing.

On an ejaculation count, the figures clearly showed the effect of viewing the pornography. On each of the 7 days preceding the experiment, an average of 19.4% of the subjects reported ejaculating. On the 6 days following the experiment, this figure was 19.7%. But on the day of the experiment itself, 49% of the subjects reported an ejaculation. (These differences were significant on a chi-square test, at probability $p < .01$.) When more details of the circumstances of these ejaculations were investigated, it became clear that they were mainly attributable to an increase in masturbation.

The conclusions were that viewing pornographic slides has the effect of making male college students masturbate more, but that this effect disappears the next day.

POSSUM
Colloquially aphetic form of opossum. See **HUMOR** (p. 136).

PREDICATE PHRASE
Defined as ''the word or words by which something is said about something,'' this would appear to cover a great deal, and may account for the popularity of predicate phrases in West Africa. See *Grammar*.

PREGNANCY
The effect of pregnancy on the contents of women's drawings is discussed in **BODIES** (pp. 103–4).

The effect of death on the pregnancy rate of mice will be found under *Death*.

PREMATURE EJACULATION
The causes and treatment of premature ejaculation in men will be found in **SEX** (pp. 73–4).

A possible treatment for premature ejaculation in dogs will be found in **ALCOHOL** (pp. 9–10).

PSYCHOKINESIS
The influence of mind power alone on physical objects. For a discussion of the psychokinetic abilities of mice, goldfish, cockroaches, lizards, rats, gerbils, philodendron leaves, algae, yeast cultures, fruit flies, drunks and a dog, see **PARAPSYCHOLOGY**.

R

RABBIT
Some useful tips on drowning rabbits will be found in **SYNCHRONIZED DROWNING** (p. 30).

A discussion and some of the lyrics of the Apache Rabbit Dance song cycle may be found in **MUSIC** (p. 125).

RACCOON
An interesting comparison between the mental abilities of raccoons and those of horses will be found under *Intelligence*.

RADISH
Whether holy water has any beneficial effect on the growth of radishes is still an open question. See **PARAPSYCHOLOGY** (pp. 149–50).

RAPE
A case of the researcher as accessory to rape will be found in **SPIDERS** (pp. 61–2).

RATS
So many rats have been of such great assistance in such a wide variety of research topics, that it is hard to know where to start. The following is a guide to where rats can be found in these pages:

For the question of whether rats can count, see *Numeracy*.

For other questions of rats' mental faculties, see *Intelligence*.

For how death can make rats pregnant, see *Death*.

A case of sudden death in rats may be found under *Voodoo*.

Mammary growth in pregnant rats may be found under *Breasts*.

Whether female rats enjoy sex may be deduced from *Orgasm*.

A result of stress in rats may be found under *Gastric ulcers*.

The deleterious effects of an unhappy upbringing on rats is

discussed under *Environment*.

Inebriated rats are found in **ALCOHOL** (p. 10).

Castrated rats are found in **SEX** (p. 80). Randy female rats are found in **COURTSHIP** (p. 96).

The sexual attraction of tennis balls for rats is found in **COURTSHIP** (pp. 95–96). Paranormal abilities of the rat are to be found in **PARAPSYCHOLOGY** (pp. 152-4).

The mealtime behavior of rats is discussed under *Sunflower seeds*.

RELIGION

In her doctoral dissertation for the Medical College of Pennsylvania: "Socialization for Body Transcendence: A Study of Elderly Religious Women," Nancy L. Kelley analysed the results of questionnaires administered to 68 retired members of the Sisters of St. Joseph, a group of Philadelphia nuns whose average age was 77.1 years.

They were given two tests called the Body Worries Test and the Body Discomfort Test. In order to test the hypothesis that a lifetime spent in a nunnery ought to enable women to transcend bodily problems, the results were compared with an earlier survey of 29 elderly secular women.

The findings, however, showed that the nuns reported more discomfort and more worry than non-nuns. Older sisters showed less worry and discomfort than younger ones. The writer stresses, however, that "caution must be used in placing excessive confidence in these findings."

More about the science-religion interface will be found in **PARAPSYCHOLOGY** (pp. 146–50) including a discussion of the effect of holy water on radishes.

RESTAURANT

A fine piece of research into restaurant behavior is reported in the December 1984 issue of *Personality and Social Psychology Bulletin*. "The Midas Touch: The Effects of Interpersonal Touch on Restaurant Tipping" by A. H. Crusco and C. G. Wetzel contains some good tips for waitresses who want good tips.

The aim of the research was to discover what effect it had on the size of tip received by a restaurant waitress if she

touched the customer on returning his change. Accordingly, waitresses participating
in the experiment touched
customers on the hand, on the
shoulder or not at all. The size
of tip, as percentage of the total bill, was taken as an objective measure of the customer's
reaction.

Results indicated that the
rate of tipping was not affected
by the type of touch (hand or
shoulder) but was significantly
higher when the customer was
touched than when not
touched at all. This result was
not affected by the gender of
the customer, holding true for
both male and female.

Customers were also asked
to complete questionnaires to
give ratings for the quality of
restaurant, atmosphere, waitress and whole dining experience. Their responses did not
indicate any effects of the
touching or nontouching waitress behavior. It may therefore
be deduced that the cause of
higher tips for touching waitresses is a purely subcon-
scious phenomenon.

A further reference to restaurants will be found in
CHICKENS (pp. 46–7).

RHESUS MONKEY
The effects of a deprived
childhood on the sexual activities of rhesus monkeys will be
found in **SEX** (pp. 85–7).

Orgasmic behavior in non-
deprived female rhesus monkeys will be found under *Orgasm*.

RHUBARB
The efficacy of rhubarb as
treatment for premature ejaculation is discussed in **SEX**
(p. 74).

RIBONUCLEIC ACID
(Abbr. RNA). See **WORMS**
(p. 51).

ROBIN
According to D. Lack ("The
behaviour of the robin II,"
Proc. Zool. Soc. London,
1939, 109, 200–219) when a
male robin attacks another
male robin, it is the redness of
its breast which brings out the
aggression. His experiments
have shown that a male robin
will attack a bundle of red
feathers, but will not attack a
dummy model of a male robin,
perfect except that the breast is
not red.

In this behavior, sticklebacks are very similar to robins. N. Tinbergen in 1951 pointed out that a male stickleback will react with fighting behavior to a red coloring on a rival male, but only if the red is on its belly, not on its back.

RUGBY FOOTBALL

A good deal of research has been done on the physiological strains affecting rugby football referees. In 1981, G. Quinn, J. A. White and J. J. Thornhill wrote "Developmental techniques for assessment of the psychophysiological demands of match officiating with reference to Rugby football league senior referees." There was then, apparently, a team change, because G. Quinn, J. A. White and C. Ward went on to write "Relationships between laboratory and field performance measurements in senior Rugby league referees."

One of their conclusions was that it is hard carrying out reliable tests on referees in the laboratory, because the stresses of actual play are far greater.

RUSSELL

(Bertrand Arthur William, 3rd Earl, 1872–1970). For Bertrand Russell's opinions on Aristotle, teeth and women, see **SEX** (p. 76).

S

SADISM
The role played by a regression to primitive sadistic themes in the popularity of video games will be found under *Video Games*.

SCHIZOPHRENIA
A potentially valuable use of spiders in the diagnosis of schizophrenia will be found in **SPIDERS** (pp. 66–8).

SCHOPENHAUER
(Arthur, 1788–1860). German philosopher who regarded Hegel as a charlatan. Schopenhauer's favorite joke, an example of rare geometric wit, will be found in **HUMOR** (p. 133).

SEDATIVES
The effect of sedatives upon spiders and their webs will be found in **SPIDERS** (p. 64).

SELF-ESTEEM
The contribution played by different parts of the body towards an individual's general self-esteem will be found in **BODIES** (pp. 109–11).

An interesting, but inconclusive, investigation into the effect of self-esteem on people's reactions to their own photographs will be found under *Narcissism*.

SEMIOTICS
The study of language and more general sign-systems of communication. For a reference to the semiotics of laughter, see **HUMOR** (p. 144).

The semiotics of TV news broadcasts will be found under *Television*.

SEXISM
According to W. A. McElroy (1954: "A sex difference in preferences for shapes," *British J. Psychology*, 45, 209–

JOSEPH CLARK *the* POSTURE MASTER.

Epistemologically speaking, semiotics was still at an empirical stage.

16): "The female form differs essentially from the male in its curved aspects, especially with respect to the full development of the breasts."

This observation helps explain a difference between boys' and girls' preferences for rounded or angular shapes. In McElroy's study, schoolchildren aged between 9 and 16 were tested for shape preferences. The results showed that boys tended to prefer rounded (female) shapes; girls chose angular or pointed shapes. The conclusion is inescapable that shape preference involves a projection of one's own sexual preferences onto the chosen objects. Girls pick boy-objects, boys pick girl-objects.

However, according to R. H. Munroe, R. L. Munroe and L. L. Lansky (1976: "A sex difference in shape preference," *J. Social Psychology*, 98, 139–40), when offered pieces of candy, in cubic or spherical packets, girls choose spherical candy, boys choose the angular sweets.

The conclusion is inescapable that shape preference involves a projection of one's own sexual identity onto the chosen objects. Girls select girl-candies, boys select boy-candies.

The whole subject clearly needs a good deal more research before a sound theoretical framework can be advanced.

More sexist behavior was identified by C. West in 1979 ("Against our will: Male interruptions of females in cross-sex conversation," *Annals of New York Acad. of Sciences*, 327, 81–97). 5 female and 5 male previously unacquainted college students were brought together for a conversation. Their contributions to the conversation were analysed in detail and a hierarchy of conversational responses was developed, varying from submissiveness to assertiveness. It was found that whereas females were just as likely to indulge in assertive conversational behavior, males were considerably more likely to interrupt females than the other way around. In fact 3 times as many male interruptions of females were found as female interruptions of males.

A sexist view of the effect of physical differences on scientific aptitudes will be found in **SEX** (p. 77).

Sex differences in musical ability among Ugandans will be found in **MUSIC** (p. 123).

SEXUAL AROUSAL
The effects of drinking on sexual arousal, and the difficulties in estimating such effects reliably, will be found in **ALCOHOL** (pp. 16-7).

The use, and deleterious side effects, of a nitrate patch to enhance sexual arousal may be found in **COURTSHIP** (pp. 97-8).

SEXUAL DEVIATION
Sexual deviation in mice, pigs, monkeys and Dutchmen will be found in **SEX** (p. 85).

Further sexual deviations will be found in **ALCOHOL** (p. 16).

SEXUAL EXPOSURE
A thematic subject area in the taxonomy of dirty jokes. See **HUMOR** (p. 135).

SEXUAL FANTASY
A discussion of the gap between fantasy and reality in the sexual experiences of newts will be found in **COURTSHIP** (p. 94).

SEXUAL INITIATIVE
It has been experimentally verified that males generally respond positively to female sexual initiatives. See **COURTSHIP** (pp. 96-7).

SEXUAL INTERCOURSE
Accounts of sexual intercourse among lions, butterflies, newts, sharks, rats,

mice, cats, dogs, guinea pigs, ducks, goats, grouse, crows, monkeys, dragonflies, chickens, spiders, goldfish, humans and other animals will be found at various places in this book. Sexual Intercourse as a joke is discussed in **HUMOR** (p. 140).

SEXUAL PERFORMANCE

The effect of drinking on sexual performance is discussed in **ALCOHOL** (pp. 16–7).

A record performance by a copulating cock (53 times in one day), is recorded in **CHICKENS** (p. 45).

For a good effort by lions (23 times in 5 hours and 20 minutes) see **COURTSHIP** (p. 91).

For a female rat with a healthy sexual appetite, see **COURTSHIP** (p. 96).

SEXUAL REFLEXES

For the effects of alcohol on the sexual reflexes of normal and neurotic male dogs, see **ALCOHOL** (p. 9).

SEXUAL RESPONSIVENESS

That an experienced female can increase the sexual responsiveness of a male of sheltered background can be found confirmed, in the case of monkeys, in **SEX** (p. 87).

SHAKESPEARE

(William, 1564–1616). Dramatist. See **ALCOHOL** (p. 7).

SHARK

For an interesting mating position for sharks, see **SEX** (p. 81).

A musical antidote to sharks will be found in **MUSIC** (p. 118).

SHAVING

The drastic effects shaving has on rats may be found under *Voodoo*.

SHRIMP

An interesting experiment involving philodendron leaves and boiling shrimps may be found in **PARAPSYCHOLOGY** (pp. 154–6).

SIAMESE FIGHTING FISH

The effects of drinking on the aggression of Siamese Fighting Fish may be found in **ALCOHOL** (p. 12).

SILENCE

A discussion of the ways in which silence can contribute to conversation was the subject of a 1975 dissertation by C. R. Meyers at the University of Texas, Austin. The title was "Silence and the unspoken: a study of modes of not speaking."

SMELL

The role of the sense of smell in the mating behavior of goldfish is discussed in **GOLDFISH** (p. 25).

The discriminatory potential of the sense of smell in dogs will be found under *Twins*.

Further smells will be found under *Vaginal Odor*.

SNEEZING

For a case of paroxysmal sneezing following orgasm, see **COURTSHIP** (p. 98).

SOAP OPERA

A revealing study into the mental processes of people who watch television soap operas was carried out for a doctoral thesis by E. Ibok at the University of Wisconsin in 1985. ("Cognitive structures and processes in recall of different types of contents on television programs.")

60 undergraduates were divided into 2 groups, depending on whether they watched day-time soap operas or not. They were then shown edited versions of television drama and soap opera and their levels of mental effort were monitored while they watched. The controversial conclusion appears to upset many traditional theories about soap opera viewers: "The results showed that subjects were mentally active during exposure to the programs."

SPARROW

A touching tale of fidelity among sparrows will be found in **COURTSHIP** (p. 94).

SPELEOLOGY

The study and exploration of caves. I thought you knew that. See **SEX** (p. 77).

SPERMICIDE

A scientific study of the efficacy of using soft drinks as spermicides can be found in **COURTSHIP** (pp. 98–100).

SPIDERS

In view of the proven potentialities of the spider to detect and identify drugs, it remains a mystery why motorists' urine samples are not fed to spiders in order to detect illicit substances. See **SPIDERS**.

SPORT

The word "sport" is an aphetic of the word "disport." For the best colors in sporting equipment, see *Squash*. For the application of mechanical principles to sport, see *Golf* and *Diving*.

For some pertinent comments on refereeing, see *Rugby Football*.

For an analysis of the relative contributions of arms and legs to sport, see *Swimming*.

For further applications of science to sport, see *Football*.

SQUASH

A 1984 Tennessee State University dissertation by M. R. Pruitt provided important information for the makers of squash balls. Entitled: "Effects of selected colors on reaction time and racquetball wall volley performance," it examines the influence of ball color on the reaction times of players of differing abilities.

. . . as a result of this study, the author suggests that green and flourescent orange racquetballs would be superior to blue during racquetball play for students enrolled in a beginning racquetball class. Furthermore, flourescent yellow, while not significantly better than blue, could prove beneficial to play.

STARLING

For a reference to aggressive behavior in castrated starlings, see **SEX** (p. 88).

STATISTICS

For the statistics about vital statistics, see **BODIES** (p. 109).

STICK INSECT

The coordination of leg movements of a stick insect were investigated in a series of papers in 1985 (*Biol. Cybern.* 51) by E. Foth and U. Baessler. The first paper was entitled "General results and 1-1 coordination." The second paper ventured into more complex areas: "Leg co-ordination when step frequencies differ from leg to leg.''

For these experiments, the stick insect was held firmly by its body, with 5 of its legs walking round a treadmill, while the sixth leg had to trot along a motor driven belt.

For anyone possibly wishing to repeat this experiment at home, we add only that it was the left hind leg which was on the moving belt.

Inconsistencies in results have been blamed on the motivational state of the experimental animals.

STICKLEBACK

For an interesting reaction to the color red in sticklebacks, see *Robin*.

For everything else about sticklebacks, the reader is referred to ''Fifty Years of Behaviour Study in Sticklebacks: Papers Read at the First International Conference on Stickleback Behaviour'' (1985) by J. van den Assem and P. Sevenster, Eds. (To be found in *Behaviour*, Vol 93.)

In one of the papers at the conference, the author comments on the less than perfect reliability of sticklebacks as experimental subjects. He suggests that the inconsistencies are due to variations in the motivational state of the fish.

STRAVINSKY

(Igor, 1882–1971). For a brief account of the reaction of pigeons to Stravinsky's Rite of Spring, see **MUSIC** (p. 118).

STUPIDITY

For some of the better points of stupidity, see *Dog*.

SUGAR

A sweet substance, $C_{12}H_{22}O_{11}$. See *Butterfly*.

SUNFLOWER SEEDS

The seeds of the sunflower. The efficacy of sunflower

seeds as gerbil food will be found in **PARAPSYCHOL-OGY** (p. 154). Their versatility, however, is demonstrated by a 1986 paper in *Animal Behaviour*, 34, 925–7, entitled "Rats prefer handling food to waiting for it."

The rats in the experiment were given the choice between sunflower seeds with husks on and sunflower seeds from which the husks had already been removed. Having previously determined the average time it takes a rat to extract the seed from the husk, the ready-to-eat seeds were made available at intervals identical to the husking time.

Thus the rats were ensured the same amount of food, whether they elected to eat the prepared seeds, or to do the work themselves. The experiment showed that they preferred the seeds with husks still on. The conclusion drawn from this was: "a seed in the paw is more certain than one in the feeder."

SUSPENDED ANIMATION
See **SYNCHRONIZED DROWNING**.

SWIMMING
A description of the leg movements of swimming ants will be found under *Ant*.

The effects of blindness, in one or both eyes, on the way goldfish swim will be found in **GOLDFISH** (p. 23).

For human swimming, an important investigation was carried out by J. Watkins (In: *Proc. Sport and Science*, 1981, by L. Burwitz, A. Lees, T. Reilly and F. H. Sanderson, Eds.) entitled "The contribution of the arms and legs to swimming speed in the front crawl stroke."

In this experiment, 26 trained swimmers (including 4 senior internationals) and 8 physical education students each swam 15 meters under 3 conditions; using their arms only, using their legs only, and full stroke. Performing front crawl using only the arms, it was found that trained swimmers can manage between 85% and 90% of their full speed. This figure was reduced slightly (78–86%) for the students, but still confirmed the relative importance of arms over legs when swimming crawl. 6 different kicking patterns were identified in the leg strokes, but no clear recommendations could be made.

Proponents of the breast stroke received no encouragement in the 1953 *British Medical Journal* (p. 1230) when a correspondent asked: "What is the best way of dealing with breasts that have become unduly pendulous after breast feeding?"

The reply was: "The most useful treatment is to ensure that the breasts are always kept well supported by a suitable brassière. Time alone will then improve matters. Exercise of the pectoral muscles—by breast stroke swimming for example—is sometimes advised, but is of doubtful value."

SYNCHRONIZED SWIMMING

The spiritual origins of this sport among the members of the Royal Chirurgical Society are to be found in **SYNCHRONIZED DROWNING** (p.29).

T

TAXIDERMY

Having one's wife embalmed is not to be recommended, according to the experiences of Martin van Butchell. This eighteenth-century eccentric had studied under the famous anatomist and surgeon John Hunter, was for many years a dentist, and later a famed maker of trusses. He was often to be seen riding in Hyde Park on a white pony, which he liked to paint sometimes purple, sometimes with purple and black spots. While riding, he carried a large white bone with which to defend himself.

On the death of his first wife, he had her embalmed by John Hunter and Dr. Cruickshank. The mummy was kept in his parlor in a glass-lidded

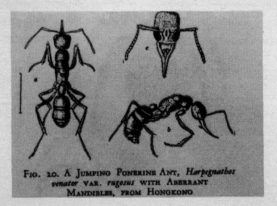

Fig. 20. A Jumping Ponerine Ant, *Harpegnathos venator* var. *rugosus* with Aberrant Mandibles, from Hongkong

If you want good mandibles, don't get them in Hong Kong.

box, where visitors were introduced to it. On his second marriage, it was found expedient to remove the body to the College of Surgeons. According to the *Dictionary of National Biography* (1886): "At the present time it is a repulsive looking object." We have no record of how Mrs. Butchell looked before her embalming.

TEETH
The question of whether men or women have more teeth is discussed in **SEX** (p. 76).

TELEVISION
An analysis of the content of television news bulletins formed the basis of a 1985 doctoral dissertation at the University of Wisconsin by D. J. Kervin entitled: "Structure and meaning: a semiotic analysis of network TV news." According to the author's synopsis:

This study suggests that while the combination of quantitative and qualitative approaches needs further refinement and application, such analysis, based within semiotics, can elicit the overt and covert meanings of messages and reveal how re-

ality is currently being structured.

This should perhaps be read in conjunction with a paper by P. C. Wason and O. Uren, entitled "The semantics of semiotics," which appeared in *New Society* in December 1974. The authors, a psychologist and a linguist, had been absolutely baffled by an article on semiotics, so conducted an experiment by sending one paragraph of that article to 49 academics to ask what it meant.

The conclusions add support to the view that anything with "semiotics" in the title is liable to be couched in impenetrably obscure, if not totally otic, language.

See *Soap Opera* for more television news.

TENNIS
To discover how to make a rat fall in love with a tennis ball, see **COURTSHIP** (pp. 95–6).

TESTICLE
According to a 1972 paper, "Afferent neural responses to mechanical distortion of the testis of the cat," by D. F. Petersen and O. Carrier Jr, squeezing cats' testicles causes

them pain. Or, to put it another way, ". . . compression in lightly anaesthetized cats indicated a pseudo-affective pain-like response to distortion of the testis." Having made this discovery, they went on to add to the knowledge with: "a glancing blow to the testicle produced a burst of activity."

TICKLING
Laughter produced by tickling is compared with laughter produced by nonphysical means in HUMOR (p. 139).

TIPPING
The behavior of waitresses to ensure better tips is to be found under *Restaurant*.

TOILET SEAT
The Ergonomics of Toilet Seats, by I. L. McLelland and J. S. Ward (Loughborough University) is perhaps the most in-depth study to date of the best way to design a toilet seat. Taking the rather brave assumption that only a seated posture would be acceptable, the researchers invited subjects to try a number of seats at different heights and angles,

with their physical and subjective responses monitored.

The definitive recommendation of the study was that the ideal height for a toilet seat is 0.4 metres. The angle of the seat was found not to be a critical factor in people's preferences. The ranges explored in the experiment were between a quarter and a half a meter for the height, and an angle of between $+6°$ and $-6°$ to the horizontal.

TOILET TISSUE
The most significant reference for research on toilet tissue is: A. Bejan (1982), "Meandering fall of paper ribbons," *Physics of Fluids*, Vol. 25, No. 5. The experiment consisted of dropping a length of lightweight toilet tissue paper and photographing its shape as it fell through the air. The research was supported by the US Office of Naval Research, but provided no guide to the effectiveness of the toilet tissue for its original purpose.

TONGA
How to dance in Tonga will be found in MUSIC (p. 125).

Degradation among handicraft sellers in Tonga will be found under *Tourism*.

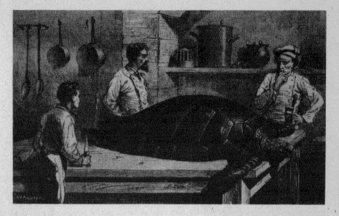

"I say we test his intelligence first, then make soup."

TONGUE

The ability of the human tongue to discriminate between holes of different size will be found under *Holes*.

TORNADO

An unsuccessful experiment to see whether chickens can be used to estimate the speed of tornados will be found in **CHICKENS** (pp. 47–9).

TORTOISE

The mental abilities of tortoises are discussed briefly under *Intelligence*.

TOURISM

The possibly harmful effects of tourism are revealed in a 1984 doctoral dissertation by D. C. Kirch at the University of Hawaii. In "Tourism as conflict in Polynesia: Status degradation among Tongan handicraft sellers" he gives the conclusions of "a comparative interactional analysis of social relations" between buyers and sellers and between sellers in both the tourist market and the local produce market. Uninformed, bargaining tourists are blamed for furthering the status degradation of the Tongans by forcing them into culturally inappropriate behavior.

TRANSVESTISM

Transvestism among poultry is discussed in **CHICKENS** (p. 43).

Transvestite chaffinches will be found in **SEX** (pp. 77–8).

The celebrated swordsman, spy, nun and transvestite, the Chevalier d'Eon.

TUBA

If you are looking for a tuba, you will find a useful catalogue of them in **MUSIC** (p. 128).

TURKEY

An experiment to discover what precocious turkeys find most sexually stimulating will be found in **SEX** (p. 84).

TURPENTINE

It is doubtful if turpentine is of much use in treating premature ejaculation. See **SEX** (p. 74).

TURTLE

See *Intelligence*.

TWINS

They may look alike, but do they smell the same? An experiment in 1955 went a long way towards answering this question. "The discrimination by the nose of the dog of individual human odours and in particular of the odours of twins" was the title of a paper by H. Kalmur in the *British Journal of Animal Behaviour* (3, 25–31).

In 1875 Francis Galton had written: ". . . it would be an extremely interesting experiment for twins who were closely alike to try how far dogs can distinguish between them by scent." Why it took 80 years before anyone did the experiment is a mystery. Perhaps it was because so many dogs had been drowned in 1862 (see **SYNCHRONIZED DROWNING** for details).

Anyway, in 1955, 17 men, 9 women, 5 children, 9 dogs and

Dogs have little difficulty tracking
Siamese twins.

36 handkerchiefs were ready to advance knowledge. Among the humans were 4 pairs of identical twins. The handkerchiefs had been specially washed, ironed and stored for a few days, being handled only by plastic forceps to ensure they were free of unwanted odors. When they came to be used for the experiments, each handkerchief would be scented for a few minutes in the armpit of one of the subjects. Some were scented on feet or palms instead of armpits, but it was discovered that ''the individuality of a person's body odour, as perceived by the dog's nose, is not greatly dependent on the region from which it emanates.''

When the handkerchiefs were used in retrieving experiments, it showed that a dog can be fooled by substituting one twin's smell for that of the other, but in tracking experiments, the dogs showed that they could distinguish between twins.

The conclusion was that the odors of identical twins, although more similar than those of other people tested, can be distinguished by well-trained dogs.

U

UGANDA
Some pertinent comments on the differences between male and females in Uganda will be found in **MUSIC** (p. 123).

UNDERCLOTHES
The reader is referred to: Ishizaki, D. B. (1952): "Bacteriological studies on the uncleanliness of underwear," *Sci. Bull. Fac. Lib. Arts & Educ.* Nagasaki Univ., 2, 24.

UNCLEANLINESS
Uncleanliness is next to ungodliness. See *Underclothes*.

UNDERTAKERS
A category of joke. See **HUMOR** (p. 135).

A physician examining urine to aid diagnosis.

URINE

For the effects on humans of drinking the urine of mushroom-eating Siberians, see *Mushroom*.

For the effects on spiders of drinking the urine of non- mushroom-eating humans, see **SPIDERS** (p. 66).

For a more flowing account of urine, the reader is referred to a book by C. C. Thomas, entitled *The Hydrodynamics of Micturition*.

V

VAGINAL ODOR

"Odor threshold and gas chromatographic assays of vaginal odors: Changes with nitrofurazone treatment," is the title of a 1970 paper (*J. Pharmaceutical Sci.*, 59, 495) by A. Dravnieks, B. K. Kroteszynski, L. Keith and I. M. Bush.

As part of their experiment, an apparatus was devised to collect vaginal vapors. A panel of observers sniffed and described the smells. The descriptions included: weak, mild, unpleasant, very unpleasant, bloodlike, strong, sweatlike, nauseating, sweet, repulsively sweet, pungent, sharp, earthy, medicinal, mushroomlike, sour, burnt, pleasant, very pleasant, and fragrant.

For another vaginal odor, see **GOLDFISH** (p. 25).

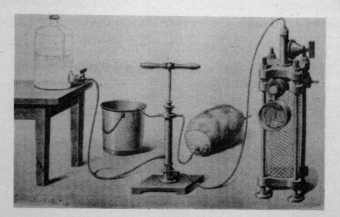

VENEREAL DISEASE
The effects of linguistic matters on the spread of venereal disease in Scandinavian countries is discussed in **COURTSHIP** (p. 98).

VIDEO GAMES
In ''The bite of Pac-man'' (1984 *Journal of Psychohistory*, 11, 395–401), M. H. Klein develops the theme that video games help adolescents regress to childhood play. Primitive oral and sadistic themes may be centered around fantasies involving a fear of engulfment. At the same time complementary aggressive tendencies may come to the surface. The popularity of Pac-man is due to its heavy emphasis on oral symbolism. The theme and strategies for the game can accommodate an adolescent's relation to the world.

VIETNAM
For a reference to double puns in Vietnamese, see **HUMOR** (p. 144).

VIRGINITY
For the effects of research on virginity in female butterflies, and the effects of virgin female butterflies on male butterflies, see **COURTSHIP** (pp. 92–3).

The attitude of virgin female spiders towards dancing is discussed in **SPIDERS** (p. 61).

VOODOO
Sudden deaths from voodoo were the motivation for a piece of rat research that resulted in a publication by C. P. Richter: ''On the phenomenon of sudden death in animals and man'' (*Psychosomatic Medicine*, May–June 1957). The author associated a remarkable piece of rat behavior with that of humans in primitive societies who die quickly after being cursed.

The rats were being used in an experiment in which the salt level of their urine samples had to be accurately measured. In order to prevent the samples from being contaminated with food dropping off the rats' whiskers, the rats were shaved. After snipping off their whiskers and trimming off their facial hair, the rats began to behave very oddly and died within eight hours.

Later, when performing another experiment, this time drowning rats to see how long they survived in water of different temperatures, the thought recurred: what happens if their whiskers are trimmed?

The answer came quickly. Whereas most tame rats can survive between 60 and 80 hours in water at 95°F, a rat with trimmed whiskers dived straight to the bottom and died in 2 minutes. 2 more shaved rats did the same. 9 further tame, shaved rats tried to spoil the experiment by swimming for between 40 and 60 hours, but 34 clipped wild rats all died within 15 minutes of being thrown in the water.

The explanation is that by having its whiskers trimmed, the rat is deprived of perhaps its most important means of contact with the outside world. This alone is disturbing enough to cause its death—as if by voodoo.

VULGARITY
How to avoid being thought vulgar while dancing in Tonga is explained in **MUSIC** (p. 123).

W

WATTLES
The effect on its sexual behavior of freezing a cock's wattles is discussed in **CHICKENS** (p. 46).

WOLF
For a description of the type of reasoning which wolves do better than dogs, and vice versa, see *Information Technology*.

WOODLICE
For a comparison of the intelligence of woodlice with that of other creatures, see *Intelligence*.

WORM
If you blindfold a chick at birth, it may grow up afraid of worms. See **CHICKENS** (p. 39).

For everything else about the flatworm see **WORMS**.

Y

YEAST
There is, at present, no evidence that yeast cultures can influence events in a paranormal fashion. See **PARAPSYCHOLOGY** (p. 154).

"Oh God! I've left the goldfish in the alcohol."

About the Author

William Hartston is an international Chess Master and former British Champion. He appears regularly as chess commentator on the BBC. Author of such classics as **Soft Pawn** and **How to Cheat at Chess**, his most recent books include **Chess: the Making of the Musical** and **The Ultimate Irrelevant Encyclopaedia**. He has an unfinished doctoral dissertation somewhere in a drawer at home.